# PRAISE FOR
## *BAIKONUR MAN*

"This is a fascinating story of an unusually risky scientific collaboration at a time of historic political and societal change. Those looking to understand a key moment that helped to advance our understanding of human biology and space flight should read this book."

—**Jennifer Doudna**, 2020 Nobel Prize Recipient, Author of
*A Crack in Creation*, and Subject of Best-Selling Biography
*Code Breaker*

"Barry Stoddard's winning new book, *Baikonur Man*, proceeds from the initial assertion that it *is* rocket science . . . but also much more: Santa Claus boxers, Armenian cognac with Russian engineers, fence building in north Idaho, rides on a Vomit Comet, grim lodgings in Kazakhstan, crystals in space . . . not to mention the collapse of the Soviet Union. For readers who want to have a little fun with their science and a little science with their fun—mission accomplished. This book is for you."

—**Keith Morris**, Editor of the *South Carolina Review*, and
Author of *Traveler's Rest* and *The Dart League King*

"Engagingly told, this book tells the fascinating story of a scientific, personal, and political journey early in the life of a young scientist thirty years ago. Its highs and lows are great and make for a terrific and timely story."

—**Richard Henderson**, 2017 Nobel Prize Recipient and
Copley Medal Winner

"Barry's book tells the story of a fascinating, high-level, and intriguing adventure. I find it hard to conceive that when so many aspects of this world seem tenuous, opposing forces can still find ways to tackle important projects for the common good."

—**Marianne Love**, Author of *Pocket Girdles*, *Postcards from Potato Land*, and *Lessons with Love*

"A great account of a young graduate student's unexpected adventures while participating in one of the very earliest experimental science projects carried out by American scientists and the Russian space program. Told with surprising frankness and down-to-earth humor."

—**Rich Roberts**, 1993 Nobel Prize Recipient and Chief Scientific Officer of New England Biolabs

"This book is both very readable and engaging! Given that much of the subject matter is beyond my limited understanding of science, that was a treat. I laughed out loud more than once, which doesn't happen very often when I read. I think the author has a hit on his hands."

— **Trish Gannon**, Editor and Author of *A Shot in the Dark: The Mysterious Death of Emma Langford*

*Baikonur Man:*
*Space, Science, American Ambition, and Russian Chaos at the Cold War's End*

by Barry L. Stoddard

ISBN 978-1-64663-942-7

Published by

**◢ köehlerbooks**™

3705 Shore Drive
Virginia Beach, VA 23455
800-435-4811
www.koehlerbooks.com

# BAIKONUR MAN

## Space, Science, American Ambition, and Russian Chaos at the Cold War's End

How Three Young MIT Students and a
Small Startup Company Snuck the First
American Payload onto a Russian Space Station
While the Soviet Union Collapsed

### BARRY L. STODDARD

VIRGINIA BEACH
CAPE CHARLES

Dedicated to Roland, Greg, Anthony, Bob, Bruce, Julianne, Sasha, Chris, and Maria. Our times together in Russia and Kazakhstan are over thirty years in the past but are as vivid for me now as when they happened.

And to Amy, Ben, and Zach, who have always supported my adventures and endured my repeated stories about them with very few complaints.

The following is a true story.

# TABLE OF CONTENTS

# PART 1:
## BEFORE THE FALL (1988 - 1990)

"Space is for everybody. It's not just for a few people in science or math, or for a select group of astronauts. That's a new frontier out there and it's everybody's business to know about it."
—Christa McAuliffe

"Our two greatest problems are gravity and paperwork. We can lick gravity, but sometimes the paperwork is overwhelming."
—Werner von Braun

"The difference between screwing around and science is writing it down."
—Adam Savage

# NORTHWEST, NORTHEAST, AND BEYOND

## Kazakhstan: December 19, 1989

**I ROLLED OVER** on the thin mattress and rough sheets of my Russian-provided guesthouse bed with considerable effort, and slowly opened one eye. A faint light was beginning to trickle through the dusty glass of my room's sole window, signaling the impending arrival of another cold, dismal morning in the military town of Zvezdograd, located in the heart of Kazakhstan. The only sound was my own congested breathing as I lay on my back and focused on a dark stain that was slowly working its way across the ceiling. Its incremental spread was clearly being nourished by damp air working its way around the room's poorly sealed window, as well as by the warmth rising from the Soviet radiator near the foot of the bed.

Moments earlier, I had been shocked into consciousness by the incessant wail of my travel alarm. Lying still in the dim light, I assessed my physical state and tried to reconstruct the previous evening. Approximately eight hours earlier, I had been pressured into an extended drinking session involving several of my American colleagues and an equivalent number of Russians. Starting briefly in a makeshift bar located near the hotel's entrance, our group decided to move the party to a nearby sauna. There, we shed our clothes until the entire group faced one another in our underwear. My boxers were printed with the large, ruddy face of a laughing Santa Claus; my wife had given them to me as an early Christmas present.

A senior official from the Russian space agency Glavkosmos produced the first of several bottles of Armenian cognac. With a wide grin, he opened the bottle with an exaggerated flourish, poured shots into a variety of glasses that had been rounded up from the kitchen, and offered a toast for the success of our mission. The details of his short speech were communicated to us with considerable effort because our company-provided translator had declined to join the group. Fortunately, a participant from each of our countries possessed a rudimentary ability to communicate in German, enabling them to pass along sentiments expressed by each side in a challenging game of drunken linguistic telephone.

The first of several highly dramatic Russian monologues poured rapidly forth from our host, emphasized by an outstretched arm holding a glass of the dark brown alcohol above his head, while he simultaneously gestured emphatically with his other hand at each of the Americans. A subsequent, far quieter exchange in halting German then took place between a red-faced Russian junior engineer and a young bearded American counterpart from our team. A tense silence permeated the sauna as the two struggled to bridge the language gap. We watched them attentively, bent forward on opposing benches with our foreheads almost touching, sweat dripping from our faces as we each clutched our own shots of cognac.

Finally, our colleague declared in English, "He said he wishes for great success and for great friendship between our groups. And that he likes your shorts."

While the most nuanced aspects of each toast were obscured by a combination of the rough translations spanning three languages and the growing effect of alcohol, the ultimate goal of bonding with one another remained well within reach.

Over the following hours, the language barrier between the groups seemed to disappear, and our speeches became increasingly eloquent, but disjointed. Friendship, brotherhood, and happiness flowed over us all. I attempted my own toast, slurring my words as I tried to express my earnest vision for future everlasting peace and happiness between our nations and their respective people. My toast sounded suspiciously like an imitation of Fred Rogers drunkenly suggesting that everyone should wish to love their neighbor. Despite that, my effort was met by upraised glasses and then downed shots.

As the bonding and shots continued, we were introduced a Russian drinking game known as "here comes the bear." The game, which was designed to accelerate our progression to complete intoxication with brutal efficiency, normally required that whenever the imaginary bear's appearance was announced ("*medvyéd prishól!*"), the party's celebrants would dive under the table and wait together until said imaginary bear was pronounced to have departed. The participants would then return to their seats for the next round of toasts. In our case, in the cramped sweltering sauna with no table to serve as a hiding place, the exhortation served instead as a signal to adjourn in an orderly manner to the neighboring dipping pool, and then cool our overheated bodies with a quick plunge into its frigid water. Retreating to the sauna, we then continued our bonding process over more shots, toasts, and return trips to the ice-cold pool.

When the cognac ran out, a quiet young Russian technician who was sporting the first wispy attempt at a mustache and had retreated to the far corner of the sauna between each round of toasts unexpectedly produced a bottle of locally distilled grain alcohol, and the drinking session continued. During the latter stages of the celebration and US-Soviet bonding, I quietly slid into a blackout state, and remaining details of the evening were forever lost. Presumably with some Russian assistance, my clothes and I were escorted back to my room and deposited onto my bed. Someone had even thoughtfully covered me with a thin wool blanket.

In the morning, probably not more than about three hours since I had been unceremoniously deposited in my room, I had no choice but to surrender to the day and the immediate need to piece myself back together. I was part of an American team sent to Kazakhstan tasked with setting up the first American research experiments destined to be launched into orbit on a Russian rocket and then placed on the Soviet *Mir* space station. The hardware for the project was being systematically assembled and loaded with samples, and we had not yet completed our work.

In terms of timing as well as circumstance, I am a product of the Cold War. I was born in the remote lumber and mining town of Libby, Montana, in February of 1963, during the frenetic early days of the Space Race and corresponding tension and ceaseless competition between the Soviet Union and the United States. Reflecting the political environment of the times and the strongly held political opinions of both my parents, I was named after Barry Goldwater, one of the most conservative and vocal anti-communist members of the United States government.

I was conceived near the end of my father's service in the US Army Corp of Engineers as both a beachmaster and as a specialist in personal nuclear demolitions. A beachmaster carries out one of the most hazardous of all combat positions; he precedes the first wave of soldiers into a landing zone immediately prior to an amphibious invasion, and then directs those troops and equipment onto and off the beach, likely while under fire from an entrenched group of defenders. The second operation has never been carried out in combat and is even more eye-opening in concept; a single individual (inserted behind enemy lines without their knowledge) would carry out the surreptitious delivery, activation, and detonation of a small hand-carried nuclear weapon and thereby destroy an industrial or military installation. Neither task seemed likely to result in a long and healthy lifespan.

My father received his honorable discharge in early October of 1962, when my mother was five months pregnant with their first and only child. On the eve of their departure from Fort Belvoir in northern Virginia, only hours after their possessions had been loaded onto a moving truck and sent away, he was contacted by his former commanding officer and informed that his discharge had been revoked. He was instructed to return immediately to his former unit, where he received maps of Cuban beaches and briefings for a possible invasion. Two days later, with my mother deposited in a roadside motel, he was on a train with fellow soldiers bound for Florida. Meanwhile, President John F. Kennedy informed the nation of the presence and threat of Russian nuclear missile launch sites located in Cuba and the possibility of an armed conflict. The Cold War was threatening to become red hot.

After thirteen anxious days that witnessed a US naval blockade of Cuban-bound Soviet ships, the downing of a US reconnaissance plane over the island, and the massing of invasion forces in Florida, the crisis ended. Mutual agreements by the USSR and the US to remove missile installations in Cuba and Turkey, respectively, and to stand down from the precipice of war enabled the two sides to back away from the unthinkable.

While the subsequent years would witness repeated conflicts around the world between agents and surrogates of both nations, it would be another sixty years before a Russian invasion of neighboring Ukraine would again raise the specter of direct conflict—and possible nuclear warfare. My father was discharged from the army for the second time in less than a month, and together with my mother proceeded on a long drive to Montana, and his first civilian job since college.

With the threat of direct military conflict between Russian and American forces reduced, the struggle between the two countries shifted back to their ongoing battle for political, economic, scientific, and technical superiority that extended back to the end of World

War II. One of the most visible of the many competitions being waged between the US and USSR was space flight and exploration. The first manned flight by Russian cosmonaut Yuri Gagarin occurred in April of 1961; it was followed shortly thereafter by a much shorter flight manned by American Alan Shepard strapped atop a US rocket. The next two and a half years would see five subsequent manned space flights launched by each country. Each flight mission was accompanied by systematic increases in both the duration and complexity.

After arriving in Montana, my father began managing a lumber and paper mill, making use of his original college degree in forestry and forest products. My parents didn't remain very long; after five years and several moves, they finally relocated permanently to northern Idaho and the town of Sandpoint in the spring of 1968. A year after our arrival, I watched Neil Armstrong take mankind's first steps on the moon while sitting on the floor in front of my parents' first color TV.

My father spent the next sixteen years working in a variety of positions for a company that pressure-treated lumber, power poles, and railroad ties. My entire childhood and adolescence were marked by forest products in one way or another, from the smell of creosote on my dad's work boots to the annual delivery of a freshly cut Christmas tree by one of the local loggers. Its arrival was always a bit of a spectacle, as it was brought to our house tied to the front of a logging truck that was already loaded with the enormous trunks of freshly harvested lodgepole pine.

Sandpoint was a small town when I was growing up. Its population was about two thousand, plus roughly that many more residents scattered throughout the surrounding area. By the late 1970s, the town was on the threshold of a transformation. While its primary economic engine had always been the timber industry and surrounding agricultural activity, tourism was on the rise. It was bordered on its south and eastern sides by Lake Pend Oreille, one of the largest and deepest bodies of fresh water in the country. To the north and west were the Bitterroot and Selkirk Mountain ranges, and with a large ski resort looming over the area, the town offered year-round recreational possibilities that were slowly altering the look and feel of its streets.

The town had two small early elementary schools located in its south and north neighborhoods, rather unimaginatively named, respectively, Washington and Lincoln. They were entirely staffed by no-nonsense elderly women with decades of teaching experience who ruled their classrooms with a mixture of strict firmness and grandmotherly compassion. Those two schools fed into a single late elementary school and adjoining middle school, and finally the area's single high school. There, I enjoyed a series of extraordinary teachers, including my physics instructor, a tall elderly gentleman with a deep commanding voice. Colonel Parker was a retired Air Force commander who had moved to Idaho and taken up education late in life. There, he enlivened his lectures with stories of how the physics of gravity and aeronautics had played out during his military career.

Included in his many tales were descriptions of parabolic "bounce flights" that he had spent a portion of his Air Force career running out of Ellington Field in Texas. Those flights were designed to provide short, reproducible periods of near-zero gravity for budding astronauts and future space researchers. To accomplish that feat, a military transport jet was flown as fast as possible while violently ascending and descending in a rollercoaster trajectory. As he explained to his students, as the plane flew over the top of each parabola or—bounce—the contents of the plane would rise and float around in the interior of the plane's cabin, due to the upward centrifugal force of the plane's path precisely balancing out the gravitational pull of the earth below. The pilots of those flights maintained the effect of zero gravity with a low-tech approach. As they flew over the top of each bounce, they adjusted their trajectory while ensuring that a plastic ball in a clear plastic tube, which was taped to the plane's console, floated between two stripes drawn near the middle of the tube.

Over the course of about two to three hours, the plane would carry out several dozen such circuits in the sky. Colonel Parker concluded his understated description, delivered in a deep baritone and slight Southern drawl, of what sounded like the world's greatest amusement ride by stating that almost everyone taking it for the first time suffered severe stomach upheaval and distress.

I had no idea, as I listened to his instruction and stories, that I would one day live through that very experience in preparation for my time as an American space research scientist.

Most of my classmates lived in the surrounding region, and many were indoctrinated at an early age into the working lives of loggers, sawmill laborers, ranchers, and farmers. While my own childhood was softer than many of my classmates, expectations of hard work still resonated in my family. My first paid job was provided by my father, who hired me at the age of ten to put a fence around our newly purchased property. We had just moved into a house a couple miles outside of town that was built on nearly an acre—not an estate, but still a fair amount of ground to surround with a fence. My father asked me if I wanted a summer job and offered me a performance-based salary of one dollar per post set into the ground. They were to be placed ten feet apart, and each was to be no less than two feet deep. By my quick estimate, the job would eventually pay well over one hundred dollars So, with dollar signs flashing in front of my young eyes, I agreed to the task without much additional thought.

Early the following Monday, the fence posts were delivered by a company truck and dumped in a pile in our yard. They were nothing other than the sawed-off ends of freshly treated, creosote-encrusted telephone poles, each one between six- and eight-feet long. My father placed a posthole digger next to the enormous pile of lumber, handed me a pair of thick leather gloves, and told me to get to work. I was instructed that each post would need to be precisely vertical and run along the edge of our property in a perfectly straight line. He then departed for his office, stating that he looked forward to seeing my progress that evening.

By the end of the afternoon, I had managed to place three posts into the ground. Aside from not realizing the sheer mass of the poles that I would be wrestling across our property, I had also not calculated that the area's soil, being the product of ancient glacial movements and forces, was peppered with large rocks that had to be excavated by hand. My father came home, briefly examined the newly implanted posts and his son (the latter covered with dirt, creosote, sweat and a little bit of blood), and declared himself to be satisfied. Reaching into his wallet, he produced three dollars.

After two more days of equally hard labor, I managed to earn another seven dollars. That evening, I approached my dad and informed him that I believed I should be paid more for my efforts. He looked up from his evening bourbon and cigarette with a slight smile on his face and asked me to tell him more. I explained that I had already put almost twenty hours of labor into the job, which worked out to barely more than fifty cents per hour. Given that the local minimum wage at that time was slightly more than a dollar per hour, a figure that had been helpfully provided to me by my mother when I previewed my case with her, I clearly deserved a raise.

My father listened patiently to my argument and agreed that I had made a solid point. He then provided me with his counteroffer; I could choose between doing the job at our originally agreed-upon level of compensation, or I could do it for free. Seeing the objections forming on my face, he asked me why I hadn't more carefully considered the work involved before taking on the job, and then inquired whether my word could be trusted or not.

Grudgingly, I agreed to keep working at the original rate. Several weeks later, the posts were all in the ground and my daily compensation had been collected. My father quietly stared at the posts surrounding our lot and asked me if I would like another job, this time stretching wire fence along the posts and around our property. "And if you want to do it," he said with a deliberate and steady gaze, "how much do you want to be paid?" Realizing that he was providing an opportunity to make up for my original poor negotiating, I suggested several thousand dollars. After a short conversation, we settled on an additional two hundred bucks.

## Kazakhstan, 1989

In ninety minutes, I would be expected to board a van with my colleagues for a half-hour ride over a bumpy two-lane road leading from our lodging to the Baikonur Cosmodrome. That facility had previously served as the launch site of Sputnik and the first man to venture into space—Yuri Gagarin. It was now destined to become the site of the first commercial and scientific American payload to be placed aboard a Russian rocket. Years of our time and effort, and significant quantities of money, company pride, and reputation, had been poured into this opportunity. It was inconceivable that I would not show up for the morning's work due to the previous evening's debauchery. Fortunately, I had been joined the night before by the president of my sponsoring company and three of its engineers, so I was not alone in my predicament.

Slowly sitting up, I realized that my fears regarding an epic hangover were misguided. While I had emerged from the previous evening's blackout, I was still quite inebriated.

I cautiously stood, still clad in my damp Santa Claus boxers. Shuffling across the room, I caught sight of myself in a floor-length mirror on the back of the door. Pausing to examine my appearance,

I noted my mottled hair, puffy eyes, and some foreign material of unknown origin on my chest. Heading toward the bathroom, I took one more glance at my sorry reflection, and then performed a slow doubletake. Turning sideways, I gingerly lifted my right arm and was rewarded by a view of a massive bruise extending from my armpit down my side and past my hip. The contusion was visibly blossoming into a spectrum of red, violet, and black. Suddenly a bit more sober, if only temporarily, I lifted my left hand and attempted a gentle assessment of the damage, softly pressing the discolored skin with my fingertips. Approximately halfway between my shoulder and my waist, I was rewarded by a sharp pain across my ribs, further lifting the thick veil of drunkenness. Through my mental stupor, I dully recognized that I had incurred a significant injury at some point during the evening's revelry.

After an unrewarding shower, I changed into fresh clothes and cautiously made my way to the dining room where the hotel staff was serving up that morning's breakfast. As I entered, a few faces turned toward me, some fresh and rested from a full night's sleep and others showing levels of stress and suffering reflective of my own. None appeared particularly concerned about my situation. The young Russian technician from the sauna, who had assisted us in setting up our portable laboratory at the Cosmodrome and later had been an enthusiastic participant in the previous night's encounter, was seated in the middle of the long dining table. He quietly gazed at me, assessing my condition with a grave expression. Suddenly, he grinned broadly, pointed in my direction, and announced my entry in two clear words of English for all who could hear—*Baikonur Man!*

By 1981, I had graduated from Sandpoint High School and accepted an offer of admission to Whitman College, where I planned to study chemistry and biology. Whitman occupied a small campus in the center of Walla Walla, a community located in the southeast corner of Washington State. It was situated in expansive rolling hills that were almost entirely dedicated to cultivation of wheat, onions, and other crops. The state penitentiary, located on the outskirts of town, added an extra source of jobs and income for the local population. Like Sandpoint, the town was on the cusp of significant change in its economics; the first of many future wineries had been established on the outskirts of the city a few years before my arrival. Walla Walla would eventually become a tourist destination, in its case driven by the existence of dozens of local tasting rooms scattered throughout the downtown and surrounding area. During my time living there, however, it was still a quiet farming community with a rural economy and conservative local politics much like my hometown.

My four years at Whitman went by in a blur, and soon I was preparing to meet my final requirements and hurdles before graduation. The college was noteworthy for confronting all its fourth-year students with a substantial challenge before they were allowed to graduate. Each member of the senior class was required to take and pass comprehensive oral and written examinations in their major. Therefore, at the appointed day and hour I presented myself in a classroom in front of four chemistry professors, who would each question me for thirty minutes in their area of interest and instruction.

This final challenge was far more than a simple formality. On occasion, unfortunate candidates for graduation were invited back to Whitman for an additional semester as a "super-senior," at their parents' expense, when they failed to pass their final exams despite multiple attempts. For chemistry majors, the object of greatest anxiety was our organic chemistry professor who had a mean streak and cantankerous demeanor, coupled with a personal viewpoint that his favorite subject should serve as a formidable intellectual barrier that would efficiently weed out the weak and unworthy from any future career in science, medicine, or academia. Most of my classmates and I had either inadvertently missed or deliberately avoided taking the class from him, a decision made possible by the timing of his sabbatical leave two years before. Now, he was back and gunning for those of us who had shown the temerity to learn the subject from a substitute professor. Suspecting this, I had spent the final month of the summer before my senior year going through the entire organic chemistry textbook and carefully reviewing the material. I had also conferred with previous graduates who provided insight into lines of questioning that he had often used as a point of attack. My strategy was simple: if asked a question that I was well-prepared for, I wouldn't stop talking, in an effort to run out the clock.

He was third in line for my examination, so I had already worked my way through almost a full hour of the exam when his time slot arrived. He gazed at me for a long moment and then removed his glasses. In a soft voice, he asked me if I could draw out the mechanism of a Friedel-Crafts acylation reaction.

*Well, fantastic*, I thought. Not only could I do that, but I had decided the night before the exam that my final choice for review and study would be exactly that, and its many variations, having been informed by a recently graduated friend that it was a topic that he seemed quite enamored with. Three minutes into my answer, he was ready to move on. I cut him off by stating that I wanted to illustrate additional aspects of the reaction with more detailed examples. He nodded, perhaps wondering where I was going with my answer. I deliberately turned my back to the panel and started to draw and describe detailed aspects of the topic on the room's blackboard. While doing so, I provided a non-stop verbal play-by-play, denying him any point of interjection. Another ten minutes were whittled away by my now incredibly detailed lecture, into which I was inserting every possible variable and tangent. When I finally turned back to the group of professors, my inquisitor's eyes had narrowed. To his sides I could see slight smiles from his colleagues. One was rubbing his temple with two fingers and looked as if he might start laughing.

The outcome of my oral exam was positive, culminating in a quiet comment from my faculty advisor. "You pretty much knew everything."

Deep into my senior year at college, and despite passing my final examinations prior to graduation, I still had little idea of what I wanted to do for the rest of my life. Like more than a few of my classmates, I delayed that decision by resolving to remain in school for as long as possible. Walking through the hallways of the science building one afternoon, I had noticed some flyers on a bulletin board for various graduate programs. Without much thought I took four and applied to each, including the Massachusetts Institute of Technology.

Returning from the holiday break for my final semester at Whitman, I stopped by my mailbox in the student center. Among its contents was a small envelope from MIT that had been posted on December 20. I opened it and read its message:

> On behalf of the Department of Chemistry, I am pleased to admit you as a graduate student and to offer you an appointment as a Teaching Assistant for the academic year 1985–1986. Under this appointment you will receive a salary of $770 each month. Your tuition of $5150 for each term will be provided as a tax-free gift.

I stared at the envelope in stunned surprise. I hadn't actually believed that I would be admitted into MIT, and beyond that skepticism nobody had ever informed me that I would be paid to continue as a student.

At the end of the summer of 1985, after a short stay in St. Louis working in a laboratory for the Monsanto Corporation, I boarded a plane with two large suitcases, bound for Boston and what seemed to me to be the center of the academic universe. Three hours later, as I stepped outside Logan Airport into the heat and humidity of a late August afternoon in Boston, I paused to observe the activity around me. A steady stream of individuals, couples, and groups collected on the sidewalk outside the terminal, heading for taxis, shuttle buses, and the parking garage. Police were blowing whistles and shouting at drivers clogging the lanes leading past the curb. To this newly arrived, small town outsider, the scene was chaotic.

My search for housing quickly became a source of concern, as it became apparent that housing in Boston, at a price that would be reasonable for a student, was almost nonexistent by the late date of my arrival. After three days of fruitless searching, I walked through the grand entrance to the Institute at 77 Massachusetts Avenue and noticed a recently posted flyer stating availability of a room in a nearby apartment. I wrote down the number and went straight to a pay phone. The tenant who had just finished posting the flyers was walking in his front door when his phone rang; he answered in a friendly manner, readily agreeing to meet with me that afternoon, stating that I was the first person to call. If he and his current roommate felt positive about me, then the room was mine. By early that evening, I had met them both and coaxed them into agreeing that I could join them. I didn't wait until the next morning to make the transition—within an hour I had moved in.

## Kazakhstan, 1989

After my entrance into the dining room was enthusiastically announced by the youngest of the previous evening's Russian participants, I slowly made my way to the long breakfast table, where I was greeted with the usual morning fare of beets, cabbage, and coffee complemented by a gristly meat of uncertain origin and vintage. I cautiously looked at my neighbors to assess their condition. The company's president had made it downstairs slightly ahead of me and  stepped outside to invigorate himself with some fresh air before sitting down at the table. Re-entering the room, he presented an interesting combination of a bald head, deathly pale face, and sunken eyes, set against two bright red cheeks generated by the cold Kazakhstan morning.

"I feel *much* better now," he quietly and unconvincingly announced to no one in particular. The lead American engineer for the project sat two chairs down from me, staring unhappily at his own plate. "Don't say a word, not one fucking word," he murmured to anyone within earshot. I turned around to one of my graduate student companions, who had also just entered the dining area. He sat beside me, eyeing me with visible irritation while also appraising my condition. He then informed me that his own fitful night's sleep had been interrupted at about 3:00 a.m. by two of us pounding on his door, hoping that he might rise from his bed and join us for the party's end.

I sighed deeply and closed my eyes, wishing unsuccessfully for a nearby Kazakh drugstore and coffee shop. The day ahead of us was scheduled to end with the final handover of our experimental payload to Russian flight engineers who would then transfer the goods into a space capsule mounted atop a Russian rocket. Eventually the materials would be delivered into the hands of two Russian cosmonauts orbiting the earth on the only game in town for space-based scientific exploration and discovery.

# TECH

**THE PROFESSOR SEATED** behind his large oak desk regarded me impassively. Dressed mostly in black, with a tight-fitting turtleneck shirt, large wire-rimmed glasses, and precisely parted hair, he provided an imposing visage to the nervous young graduate student seated in his office. Suddenly and unexpectedly breaking into a broad smile, he greeted me enthusiastically. "I remember your application! I told everyone on our admissions committee we had to let you in. How could we not take a kid from some little hick town in the middle of Idaho?"

I was sitting in the office of Dr. Gregory Petsko, a young, energetic assistant professor who had been recruited to join the chemistry department at MIT only a few years earlier. A few weeks after my own arrival in Cambridge, gripped by increasing anxiety over identifying a suitable project and willing supervisor for PhD training, I had requested an appointment to speak to him about his research and the possibility of joining his laboratory. Within thirty minutes of our introduction, I had become convinced that I should rethink what I might study and accomplish during graduate school and had decided to join his research group. The future trajectory of my entire scientific career and life had been decided in the same amount of time that I might have previously devoted to watching a rerun of *The Twilight Zone*.

The Massachusetts Institute of Technology, simply referred to as "The Institute" or "Tech" by its students and staff, was founded in 1861, with the signing of its charter corresponding closely to the start of the Civil War. The vision for the Institute, both then and now, was to create a premier academic institution to promote rapid scientific and technological advancement. After a four-year delay, its first classes were opened to students in rental space in Boston in 1865. After decades of growth and academic evolution, marked by early financial difficulties and multiple attempts at hostile takeovers by Harvard University, the Institute moved across the Charles River to a large new campus in 1914. Built on a long tract of landfill, the MIT campus grew to dominate the riverbank that faces Boston's Back Bay neighborhood.

MIT has always been intimidating and exciting for those who enter it, with demands on the academic abilities of its students that were legendary and, for many of its newest arrivals, overwhelming. When I arrived, MIT was in the process of switching to a grading system in which all first-semester freshmen would be subject to simple pass/fail grading, rather than the traditional grade range of A to F, to reduce their worries about grades and competition. The mental pressure on the students—both real and self-imposed—was immense. They had all climbed to the very top of their high school class rankings and had experienced nothing but previous academic success and accolades. At MIT, many of the gifted would suddenly struggle in their classes for the first time. Most readjusted their expectations quickly, realizing that to be anywhere near average by Tech's standards would be perfectly fine. A minority, however, struggled greatly with MIT performance anxiety. When I arrived, the Institute was struggling to address student depression and had recently been rocked by several suicides.

The response from the student body was variable and could sometimes be cold. MIT legend held that years before, in response to several closely timed deaths on campus in which students had jumped off the Institute's tallest building (Building 54, known as the Green Building), their classmates had painted a short-lived target on the pavement below, with the concentric circles labeled from an *A* in the bullseye to an *F* at the periphery. An extension of those stories went on to state that upon instituting the less stressful pass/fail grading system for first-semester freshmen, an alternative target for first-year students had appeared on the opposite side of the building, with only a single large circle indicating a pass. While perhaps apocryphal, these stories were nonetheless accepted by many as an entirely reasonable representation of the MIT academic culture.

The original buildings at the center of campus form an imposing series of neo-classical structures surrounding a central great dome and facing across the Charles River towards Boston's Back Bay neighborhood. Several of those buildings are inscribed with the names of prominent scientists from the annals of scientific history and discovery. My own laboratory took its place in Building 2, directly under the name of Louis Pasteur. That building would be my academic home during the next five years of my PhD training.

The varying integrity and unreliable quality of the reclaimed landfill that MIT rests upon was readily evident to the naked eye. Various haphazard concrete ramps had been added to the connections between many of the adjoining structures to accommodate the uneven settling that had occurred over the decades.

Connecting many of those buildings was the "infinite corridor," a quarter-kilometer long hallway running east to west. I was greeted my first day on campus by an extensive student prank, (known as a "hack" by the MIT community), in which the entire corridor had been transformed into a spoof of the nearby Massachusetts Turnpike. The hallway had been renamed the "Massachusetts Toolpike" to acknowledge the Institute's student population, many of whom were referred to as "tools," and their penchant for intense studying as "tooling." The hallway was now a pedestrian thoroughfare complete with traffic signals, direction signs, lane markings, and even parked cars.

That hack was extremely tame by MIT standards, the latest in a long history of practical jokes large and small directed at the Institute. Such hijinks injected levity into the gravitas of the college while demonstrating technical prowess on the part of the hackers, as well as a sense of humor and commentary on life at the Institute. One of the most famous MIT hacks was the placement of a replica of a police car on top of the MIT great dome with its lights flashing. A dummy of a campus police officer, seated at the wheel next to a supply of coffee and donuts, completed the installation. The license plate on the car read *IHTFP*, an acronym corresponding to MIT's unofficial student slogan—"I Hate This Fucking Place."

Near the end of my time at the Institute, a different hack illustrated a reality of life for the students—a firehose and concrete-embedded fire hydrant had been connected to a drinking fountain in Building 16. Anyone who had trained at MIT instantly recognized the significance of the installation; obtaining your education at Tech was a lot like taking a drink from a firehose—the stream of material and information was intense and unrelenting.

During their time in Cambridge, many MIT students engaged in a subtle ritual to further illustrate and define their relationship to the Institute. They would purchase an MIT class ring, which had an engraving of a crouching beaver, also known as nature's engineer, on its top surface. During their time as students, they would wear the ring with the beaver's ass pointing up their arm and towards their own body in silent acknowledgment that MIT was continuously shitting on them. Upon graduation, they would turn the ring around and point the beaver's ass outward, so that it could then shit on the rest of the world.

As of my writing this chapter, MIT has been home to ninety-six Nobel Laureates, eighty-eight winners of the National Medals of Science or Technology and Innovation, seventy-seven MacArthur Fellows, and fifteen Turing Award winners. Its halls and rooms provide visual testimony to its unceasing history of discovery and research.

The list of innovations that arose from MIT span items ranging from the first wind tunnel, developed and used at MIT in 1896, to ultra-rapid photography capturing images such as bullets caught in the act of piercing apples or lightbulbs, and modern lithium-ion batteries. The process leading to colorized movies and television shows was invented by MIT graduates and named "Technicolor" in honor of the Institute. Many products that we now take for granted, including condensed soup, disposable razors, transistor radios, and electronic spreadsheets, trace their origins to MIT. Companies including E-Trade, Hewlett-Packard, and Bose similarly locate their origin stories, in whole or part, at MIT. Radar technology was perfected in the MIT "Rad Labs" and hastened victory for the Allies in World War II. Then as now, a sense of creation, accomplishment, and potential was palpable every day throughout the campus.

On my first day at the Institute, I reported to the chemistry department, known then and now as "Course 5." Much like its buildings, the departments and majors at MIT were referred to by numbers: chemistry was Course 5, biology was Course 7, mechanical engineering was Course 2, and so on. For my first semester, I was assigned to work as a graduate teaching assistant in the freshman-level general chemistry labs, where I would team up with another member of my entering graduate class to provide hands-on instruction to sections of about thirty undergraduates as they worked through the laboratory curricula. I quickly realized what these teenage students, only four years younger than myself, were facing; the entire incoming first-year class was required to take a year's worth of college-level general chemistry in a single semester, and then follow it with the equivalent of a full year's organic chemistry class the following semester. For these students, the firehose was wide open and dispensing knowledge and education in a torrent.

Despite the intensity of both the curricula and the students, I immediately found my students to be entertaining, interesting, and enjoyable. Whereas many of them had never been anything remotely like one of the cool kids in high school, at MIT they suddenly found themselves on a new, level social playing field. Extraordinary intellect or unusual and quirky personal identities and social demeanors were just as likely to be admired as not. Acting as their instructor was a considerable challenge intellectually. I dove into textbooks more intensely than I had during my own undergraduate years, lest I be brought up short by the questions—and answers—thrown at me by my highly intelligent charges. I followed up my first semester as a lab teaching assistant by running classroom recitation sections for the spring semester organic chemistry course—hour-long, early morning sessions in which groups of twenty to thirty students tried to assimilate the torrent of information provided during full-class lectures by the class professors, with the assistance of graduate students. I enjoyed the experience so much that when I was asked to do it again near the end of my time in graduate school, I gladly consented.

Finding a home in the Petsko lab for my PhD studies was not my original plan. I had not spent much time planning or thinking about future research training, preferring to let fate dictate my future. Knowing that I hoped to work at the boundary of biology and chemistry, I initially seized on the idea that I would join the lab headed by one of MIT's many Nobel laureates, a professor whose work helped lead to the determination of the genetic code— the sequence of DNA bases in an organism's chromosomes that correspond to the sequence of amino acids in protein molecules. In the mistaken belief that joining his laboratory as a first-year graduate student would simply be a matter of asking politely, I made an appointment to meet the great man. Within mere minutes, my pitch was met with a quiet, visibly unenthusiastic response of "not possible." I left his office confused and discouraged.

Subsequent visits to other faculty were more positive but had failed to stir much excitement in me. I was starting to feel some anxiety about how things were progressing. Finally, I found myself in the office of one of the younger faculty members in the department, Dr. Greg Petsko. He was a practitioner of the scientific discipline of protein crystallography, which was the primary approach being used to visualize the three-dimensional structures, atom by atom, of biological molecules found within all living cells and organisms. Although the method had been employed successfully for almost thirty years at that point, the determination of the structure of a protein molecule, most of which contained many thousands of individual atoms, was still formidable. As of 1985, a person could still count the number of completely unique protein structures on his or her fingers and toes, and a single afternoon in the library with a stack of quarters could produce a personal binder containing photocopies of most of the important published papers describing such structures.

In Greg's office, he treated me to a one-man dramatic performance as he described the unlocking of a protein's secrets of form and function through X-ray crystallography, and the magnitude of accomplishment that one would inevitably enjoy by contributing to the field. His voice rose and fell in a spellbinding cadence as he rapidly described the many projects he was interested in pursuing. At one point he had risen from his chair and pointed his arm at me as he made his point, and then crashed back into his seat and lowered his voice to a conspiratorial whisper. As a fellow trainee in Greg's lab later mentioned to me over the first of many future beers, "If you had a time-averaged photo of Greg describing his research to a potential new student, he would look like Patton on the eve of battle."

After thirty minutes, I had been thoroughly seduced, and my mind was forever made up. I would join the Petsko lab and learn to solve structures of the most awesome molecules ever created. I would follow Greg and his lab into battle regardless of the challenges involved.

# SEEING ATOMS

**I CAME TO** realize that I was not the only graduate student who had succumbed to the persuasive skills of Greg Petsko and was not the first to recognize that success in his lab required the ability to distinguish between his brilliance, which was formidable and always worth one's full attention and subsequent action, and his occasional flights of fancy. One postdoctoral fellow, who occupied a desk in the lab immediately outside of Greg's office, had purchased an ancient hand-cranked toy steam shovel at a flea market and had placed it on a shelf by the doorway separating the two spaces. He informed us that he had positioned it there to be ready to scoop up any bullshit that might flow out of our leader's office. When students were being held as captive audiences in that space, the postdoc would sometimes quietly reach up and turn the crank on the toy, thereby inducing its well-oiled scoop to swing through the air slowly and silently. With the steam shovel fully visible to the students sitting on Greg's couch, but blocked from our leader's vision from around the corner and behind his desk, its activation resulted in desperate attempts to stifle open laughter as our boss continued his latest dramatic monologue.

My lab mates were a diverse group, featuring a collection of graduate students working toward their doctoral degrees, augmented by a few older postdoctoral fellows who were one final step away from competing for faculty positions around the world. The Petsko lab had already produced a couple individuals who were now running their own research laboratories; we all aspired to follow in their tracks. After joining the lab, I had been swiftly accepted into the group dynamic, which involved a combination of competitive egos, demanding projects, and a daily ritual of sarcastic commentary about politics, sports, and society. Several of my fellow students were lifelong natives of the East Coast and expressed outlooks about life that were more caustic and cynical than what I had experienced in the easygoing Pacific Northwest. One had been raised in an apartment building near Harlem that housed three times as many human beings as the entire town that I had grown up in.

Many days concluded with a stroll to the neighboring Walker Memorial Building, where a pub named the Muddy Charles offered inexpensive beer, snacks, and the opportunity to continue dissecting the day's events. In one of my first drinking sessions there, a staff scientist in the chemistry department's shared X-ray facility, a brilliant, but gruff and rather profane Australian, questioned me about myself and my project, while offering his unsolicited opinions on any aspect of MIT life that occurred to him. A recently tenured professor in a neighboring department? "A total wanker." The seasonal New England lager on tap that evening? "Raw sewage."

I tried to keep up as he opined about science, politics, society, the Institute, Greg Petsko, and my origins from the rural American West. "You sound like a bloody bogan." My laboratory companions came and went, listening to the conversation with variable degrees of interest and occasionally adding their own zingers. Well into the evening, he suddenly looked up from his pint and fixed me with a piercing gaze. "By tomorrow neither of us is going to remember any of this," he stated emphatically in his loud Australian accent, waving one arm at the surrounding bar patrons for emphasis.

Coming from the conservative environment of Whitman College, where student drinking was deeply frowned upon by the administration (yet enthusiastically pursued by the student body), I found the concept of a bar located in the middle of a college campus to be revolutionary. The Muddy was one of two bars located on the grounds of MIT; staff and students located on the west side of the Institute could save themselves a walk and instead enjoy their drinks at the Thirsty Ear. Our own lab bounced back and forth depending on our mood.

My first year in graduate school moved rapidly. I was simultaneously teaching undergraduates, taking my own graduate level courses in biophysical chemistry, and learning about the research projects that Greg had pitched to me in our first office meeting. I had been provided a desk in the lab, but quickly found out that bench space for actual experiments, as well as basic lab equipment, was in short supply. Much of the hands-on experimentation being done in the lab, other than collecting X-ray data and then spending weeks in front of a computer terminal, involved little more than dispensing purified protein samples that had already been provided to us by distant collaborators, ready to go, into crystallization trays. I ended up spending my entire graduate research career using a small fume hood for the few experiments I conducted that actually required test tubes or beakers.

I was assigned three projects in rapid succession, with the expectation that I would multitask my way into success on at least one of them. All three involved trying to determine the atomic structure of a protein and then use that information to try to understand how it functioned in a living organism.

In due time, I grew to appreciate this style of science. Success in a laboratory on any one project is entirely unguaranteed, regardless of effort and intelligence; sometimes a molecule simply will not give up its secrets willingly. Furthermore, even when a problem can be solved, there is no promise that it can be done in a timeframe corresponding with the length of a reasonable graduate student career. I had no wish to still be working towards my doctoral degree as I approached my thirties, so the opportunity to put multiple projects and problems into play and then to run with whichever one worked out was clearly to my advantage. I would eventually continue this same operational model when I ran my own research laboratory; all of my students would work on multiple problems.

One of my more jaded and hyper-focused faculty colleagues at the Hutchinson Center in Seattle, where I eventually came to reside for the remainder of my career, would describe this style of science with open skepticism. Over a beer late one afternoon he likened my research strategy to a blind man firing a shotgun into the sky in the middle of the night, hoping to hit something. This was not an unfair analogy, but nonetheless this style of research has always worked well for my lab and myself.

X-ray crystallography is nothing more than a version of microscopy, in which an image of something extremely small (in our case, a protein molecule) is magnified to the point that an investigator can visualize its exact three-dimensional structure, one atom at a time. When learning the approach and how to do it, the starting points of understanding the technique are obvious. Why use X-rays, and why grow crystals of the protein molecules? I always pose the same two questions to students today; the answer to both lies in the interaction of light with matter.

In almost any form of microscopy, a beam of light is shined upon the object being examined, and then the scattered light from that object is refocused by a lens onto a detector (your own retina if you are looking with your eyes through a typical microscope, or a sheet of film or a camera when using a fancier microscope). Visible light is simply a form of electromagnetic radiation, which travels through space acting as a wave; all waves have amplitudes (how high and low the peaks and troughs of the wave are) and wavelengths (the distance between two consecutive waves). Other forms of electromagnetic radiation (electrons, X-rays, gamma-rays, ultraviolet) are also forms of light, with wavelengths that differ greatly from the visible light that we can see with our own eyes.

An important principle of microscopy is that the distance between sequential waves of the light being used should be roughly the same as the distance between any two features within the object that you wish to distinguish from one another. In the case of a protein molecule, we want to be able to see groups of individual atoms; the distances between them range from a little more than one angstrom to several angstroms. One angstrom, abbreviated with an $\mathring{A}$ symbol, corresponds to one ten-billionth of a meter. To see the atoms within a molecule, we need to shine a light on it with a wavelength of no longer than one to two angstroms. X-rays meet that requirement.

So, X-rays are simply a form of light that have wavelengths that are appropriate for visualizing molecular structures at atomic resolution. So then, why do we need crystals?

The answer to this question arises from the need to amplify the signal in an X-ray experiment. The intensity of an X-ray scattered from a single protein molecule is too weak to measure accurately. Therefore, what is needed is a strategy to place many millions of identical copies of the protein molecule in front of an X-ray beam simultaneously, with the molecules being held together in precisely defined arrangements in order to amplify the scattered X-rays. A crystal of the molecule satisfies the need to act both as a molecular organizer, such that all molecules are packed into an array of repeating rows and columns, and as an amplifier because the scattering of X-rays from all the molecules in the crystal build upon one another to create patterns that can easily be measured.

The resulting data, called "diffraction patterns," corresponds to spots on a detector. After measuring the darkness of each spot generated from a protein crystal, investigators can use a variety of approaches—hopefully accompanied by a fair amount of luck—to produce a three-dimensional image of where the atoms are, which allows them to model the structure of the protein.

That, at least, was the idea. In the late 1980s, the practice was much more difficult.

It has been argued that protein crystals are perhaps the most valuable substances by weight that have ever been created by humankind, a claim with considerable merit and the numbers to back it up. Our laboratory had a cartoon posted on a wall. In it, a wizened guru was speaking to his acolyte, stating, "Forget enlightenment . . . I want you to solve the structure of a protein."

The punchline of that comic was not far from the truth. At that time almost every solved protein structure was the product of years of hard labor with no guarantee of success. The rewards for doing so at that time were immense - an immediate combination of visible envy and heartfelt congratulations from your lab mates, the sudden admiration and respect of faculty, a guaranteed doctoral degree, rapid invitations to conferences and seminars, and almost automatic consideration for a future university faculty position. Beyond that, the potential value of protein structures for medicine and biotechnology was becoming increasingly clear. Armed with such information, investigators might be able to design small molecules that could interact with the protein in a manner that prevented its function—i.e., a drug. That concept was referred to as "structure-based drug design."

The concept of turning protein structures into valuable new drugs was foremost in the minds of many who worked in the field in the late 1980s. At that time scientists were engaged in feverish efforts to create new drugs and treatments against human diseases, particularly those that could block the ability of the human immunodeficiency virus to cause AIDS. During my time at MIT, the first X-ray crystal structures of a key protein from HIV were determined by scientists at the National Cancer Institute. A book written shortly thereafter by Barry Werth, entitled *The Billion-Dollar Molecule: The Quest for the Perfect Drug,* detailed the near-maniacal efforts of a local startup company to use that information to generate new antiviral drugs. Each of us in the lab read it in turn, laughing at its description of the company's research scientists, located just up the street from us, working at the edge of professional and personal breakdowns as they strove to be first to achieve that goal.

While all the steps of solving a protein structure were challenging, the key step was to turn a solution of a purified protein into well-ordered crystals containing the same protein molecules. This process required an amalgamation of effort, knowledge, skill, intuition, and perhaps some black magic. The protein being studied needed to be purified to almost perfect homogeneity, free of contaminants—no small feat in and of itself. After being purified, the protein needed to exist almost entirely in one discrete shape and size to have even a remote chance of crystallizing; an investigator had relatively few tricks available to dictate such desired behavior. Finally, the protein, which was dissolved in water and perhaps a bit of various salts, had to be coaxed into leaving its aqueous surroundings in favor of joining together with copies of itself in a crystalline lattice.

The ways in which one might accomplish the process of protein crystallization were almost countless, and there were no obvious rules leading a researcher to know which strategy to employ. Crystallization was usually accomplished by slowly introducing other molecules—more salts, sugars, acids, bases, oils—into the protein solution in a way that slowly increased their concentrations. During that process, those molecules would compete for surrounding water with the protein, until finally there wasn't enough to go around. At that point, one of the components (hopefully the protein) would self-associate and remove itself from solution. Under perfect but quite unpredictable experimental conditions, that process would result in the formation of a protein crystal. Usually measuring no more than a millimeter on each side, the generation and validation of a new protein crystal was greeted by all in the lab with a mix of excitement, respect, and jealousy.

The number of variables that needed to be systematically tested to find the right conditions for protein crystal growth were overwhelming. Some obvious candidates were the starting concentration of the protein, the volume of the drop containing the protein, and the way that additional molecules were slowly added. The number of different compounds and additives that could be tried as crystallization reagents were truly limitless. If the protein was known to tightly bind a small molecule, then that had to be tried as well. The temperature in the laboratory was another key variable, as were the glass or plastic trays used. The vibration in the building was also thought to be important. An outbreak of dandruff on the day that crystal trays were being set up might easily affect the crystallization process.

Finally, in my opinion the mental outlook and confidence of the researcher was critical. I always whispered to my experiments as I put them away on my lucky shelf—the one spot in the lab where I believed crystal growth was optimal. "You're going to be awesome."

All the lore, technique, superstition, and insight into protein crystallization became part of my scientific training during graduate school, as well as the most important step of what I was trying to accomplish. After my first year, I was making slow but steady progress, having crystallized two of the proteins that I was working on for my thesis project. I was still in the early days of learning what it meant to be a structural biologist, but things were moving along. Little did I know that several months before, a catastrophe that had gripped the entire nation would change the direction of my research training and my life.

# "OBVIOUSLY A MAJOR MALFUNCTION"

**THE MORNING OF** January 28, 1986 was, like most winter days in Cambridge, uncomfortably cold, just below freezing when I walked into the Institute from my apartment, with scattered snowflakes circling me in a brisk wind. My eyes watered as I strode down Massachusetts Avenue with my head down and my jacket collar up.

I had not expected to feel so chilled by simple winter weather when I came to the Boston area. Having grown up at elevation in the Idaho panhandle, I was comfortable with snow and heavy winter storms. I quickly found, however, that the type of cold encountered on the coast of New England during the winter months was a different beast. The air was exceedingly damp, and the wind funneled between buildings and raced down the sidewalk, converging on my exposed face. The difference between winter air and snow where I grew up, which had usually been scrubbed of a considerable amount of excess moisture by preceding coastal mountain ranges before it arrived farther inland, versus the climate in coastal Massachusetts was considerable. Whereas a younger version of myself had relished spending his winter days outside, in Cambridge my enjoyment of cold weather was greatly diminished.

The freezing temperatures that day on the East Coast were not limited to the Northeast. A cold front had descended onto much of the seaboard and all the way to the southern tip of the state of Florida; an overnight low of 18°C in Miami had still not risen above freezing by late morning. On a launch pad at the Kennedy Space

Center, the *Challenger* space shuttle and its crew awaited liftoff. They were unaware that the cold weather would soon conspire with years of critical errors in judgement and more recent failures in communication to cause the greatest disaster in the history of the American space program. The failure and deaths that morning would lead to years of recrimination and guilt, as well as an immediate shutdown of the American manned space exploration program for almost the next three years.

STL-51-L was the twenty-fifth mission of the Space Shuttle program. That morning, the *Challenger* shuttle carried seven crew members, including Michael Smith, Gregory Jarvis, and Christa McAuliffe, who were embarking on their first spaceflight. McAuliffe, a teacher living and working in Concord, New Hampshire, was a true New England native, born in Boston and raised in nearby Framingham. She had been chosen to be the first civilian and American teacher in space. She had emerged from the applicant pool for the Teacher in Space Project as the chosen individual who would engage with students and fellow educators while in orbit. Her fellow crew members were from many points around the country. Ronald McNair was a South Carolinian who had earned a PhD in physics from MIT ten years earlier in the field of laser physics. Multiple objectives awaited the crew once in orbit, including deployment of a weather-tracking satellite, activation of another satellite to be focused on Halley's Comet, and opportunities for student teaching.

Also included in the mission payload and objectives were equipment and protocols to examine the effect of zero gravity on fluid dynamics—how weightlessness would affect the properties and behaviors of a range of different liquids during various types of mixing and handling processes. Such data was important for a wide range of possible scientific and manufacturing processes. One such application, of considerable interest both to NASA and to the biotech community (including myself and my lab mates), was the growth of protein crystals, which required that various liquid solutions be brought into proximity or contact with one another and allowed to equilibrate.

As early as 1983, the US space program had begun to fly protein crystallization experiments aboard the shuttle and had begun promoting the potential of zero gravity (on which NASA had a near-monopoly) to grow bigger, better crystals. There was little doubt that if space flight could deliver success in growing better crystals and help investigators to solve the structures of new and otherwise inaccessible proteins, the pharmaceutical industry would consequently beat a path to NASA's door with their checkbooks in hand.

After arriving at the Institute at about 9:00 a.m., I had started what promised to be a busy day. MIT was nearing the end its Independent Activities Period, or IAP, which ran through the month of January. The IAP provided an opportunity for MIT students and faculty to participate in a variety of non-graded symposia, workshops, arts and athletics, contests, and social activities. It also provided a chance for students and staff alike to prepare for the onslaught of the upcoming semester. I was scheduled to work as a teaching assistant in the organic chemistry class, during which a year's worth of information and material would be crammed into the brains of returning freshmen over about twenty weeks. I was scheduled to lead two consecutive morning recitation sections of about twenty to thirty students each, and I was already working ahead in the MIT text and problem sets to try and stay a step ahead of much smarter individuals than myself.

Late that morning, I was walking through the infinite corridor to a scheduled meeting with one of my faculty advisors. I slowed under the Great Dome; as usual a crowd of students was congregated at the Institute's ground zero, socializing as they slowly worked their way towards various destinations. I noticed that an overhead TV was broadcasting the impending launch of the *Challenger*. Not surprisingly, students' eyes were trained on the images being transmitted from Florida; the impending launch mission was the type of event that drove almost any self-respecting member of Tech into a science nerd overload. I was certainly among them. While I wasn't involved in the study of aerospace engineering or space flight technology, I had grown up in the era of *Apollo*, the moon landings, and *Skylab*, and still found TV coverage of the US space program captivating.

I walked into the lobby within a minute or two of the scheduled liftoff and paused to watch. As the countdown progressed, I heard commentary that the launch had been significantly delayed due to cold temperatures in Florida. As the boosters ignited and the shuttle rose off the launch pad and then gathered speed over the next minute, there seemed to be nothing out of the ordinary to the start of the mission. I reshouldered my backpack and prepared to continue my day. Just as I took my eyes off the screen, a loud synchronized gasp followed by silence emanated from the group of students still watching the broadcast.

Looking up at the screen, it was immediately obvious that something had gone terribly wrong. The carnage from an enormous explosion was clear to all. The screen was filled with smoke, debris, and contrails curling through the sky from the suddenly liberated rocket boosters. Forgetting everything that had been in my mind only a moment before, I stared at the screen in shock. For several seconds there was no sound from the crowd and little commentary from the broadcast. Then, a simple statement issued from mission control. "Flight controllers looking very carefully at the situation . . . obviously a major malfunction."

As the cause of the *Challenger* disaster was investigated and examined, the extensive connection between the US space shuttle program and MIT came into sharp focus. Multiple companies involved in the design and fabrication of the rocket boosters and the shuttle were connected to research and development performed at the Institute. Many of the scientific payloads committed to launch involved MIT labs and their investigators. An MIT-trained scientist was among the mission specialists on the shuttle that morning. Three separate members of the Rogers Commission, which was charged with investigating and reporting on the disaster, were MIT alumni. One of them, Dr. Eugene Covert, was the current chair of the Institute's Department of Aeronautical and Astronautical Engineering.

The commission's final report detailing the events and decisions leading up to the loss of the shuttle and its crew was damning. The accident itself was traced to the failure of O-rings at a joint on the right solid rocket booster, which allowed the escape and ignition of superheated gases, resulting in the structural failure and eruption of the external fuel tank. That failure in turn was connected to an underlying design flaw, in that the performance (and possible failure) of that assembly was strongly dependent upon external environmental factors, most prominently low temperatures that could degrade the mechanical sealing properties of the O-rings. Engineers at the rocket contractor Morton Thiokol had raised the issue with their counterparts at NASA multiple times throughout the ten years preceding the *Challenger* disaster, but the issue had not been elevated to the level of an actual redesign of the system. Instead, senior staff on the NASA launch team had decided to treat the issues as a parameter that could be managed as an acceptable risk. In the final twenty-four hours before the launch and explosion, NASA officials and Morton Thiokol engineers and executives had debated if the cold weather might cause a potential catastrophic failure. After initially agreeing to postpone the launch, the decision was reversed, with NASA executive Lawrence Mulloy infamously stating, "My God, when do you want me to launch . . . next April?"

The night before the launch, as he prepared for bed, one of those same Morton Thiokol engineers matter-of-factly stated to his wife, "It's going to blow up."

The most prominent member of the investigating committee,

famed physicist Richard Feynman, was highly critical of NASA, stating that they had failed to correctly estimate and act upon risk and reliability of the launch system, a failure that he linked to a lack of attentiveness by their management to the recommendations of the engineers who were most familiar with the frailties of the system. It was revealed that the unanimous recommendation by Morton Thiokol engineers to delay the launch (during a conference call with NASA managers at Kennedy Space Center and the Marshall Space Center the night before the scheduled launch) was ignored and overridden both by NASA and by Thiokol management. The Rogers Commission concluded that the *Challenger* disaster was an "accident rooted in history" stemming from an initial faulty engineering design to subsequent failure to recognize the potential risk inherent in that flaw, to a final decision to forgo fixing it and instead treating it as an acceptable and manageable flight risk.

Nearly twenty years later, Kenneth Iliff, who had worked on the X-15 hypersonic rocket aircraft program and then on the Shuttle program since its inception, stated, "Not violating flight rules was something I had been taught on the X-15 program. It was something that we just never did. We never changed a mission rule on the fly. We aborted the mission and came back and discussed it. Violating a couple of mission rules was the primary cause of the *Challenger* accident."

The sudden grounding of the US Shuttle program thrust the Soviet Union into a sudden position of enjoying a monopoly on manned space flight and corresponding scientific activities beyond the limitations of Earth's gravity. Only three weeks after the *Challenger* explosion, the core block of the *Mir* space station was launched into orbit from the Soviet rocket base located in Baikonur, Kazakhstan. One month later, in mid-March of 1986, Leonid Kizim and Vladimir Solovyov became the station's first residents, spending fifty-one days in orbit bringing the station online. From that point onward, until its final days and spectacular atmospheric burn-up in a planned descent fifteen years later, the station would be manned almost every day of its existence.

That the Russians could effectively compete with the US and its allies for supremacy in manned space flight, even after the Americans' success in the race to the moon, was not surprising. Soviet work on rockets and space flight had begun shortly after the end of the First World War, in 1921, with important contributions that included the first detailed proposals for the development of multi-staged rockets and for lunar orbit rendezvous. After the end of the Second World War, while Russian space scientists labored to develop military rockets capable of delivering nuclear warheads between the Euro-Asian and North American continents, multiple competing programs began to also work, mostly in secret, on developing manned space-flight capabilities.

The first successful launch and recovery of live animals was achieved by the Soviets in 1951, followed in 1957 by the launch of *Sputnik-1* and in 1961 by the first man in space, Yuri Gagarin. Throughout the years between the launch of *Sputnik-1* and the assembly and manning of the *Mir* space station, the Soviet Union would rack up dozens of space flight and exploration firsts, including interplanetary probes, women in space, multi-person flight crews, unmanned moon landings and exploration, and hosting of crew members from highly diverse nationalities and ancestries.

In 1987, the Soviet space program would record another first, when two cosmonauts, Vladimir Titov and Musa Manarov, became the first crew to spend over one continuous year in space while manning *Mir*. Only a few months later, the same space program would agree to host American experiments aboard the same orbiting platform, to the immense surprise of space scientists, politicians, and leaders throughout the US and the USSR. Three young MIT graduate students, including myself, would suddenly find themselves at the front and center of that project.

# FIRST CONTACT

## February 4, 1988

**I HAD JUST** arrived at the lab, removed my coat, and sat at my desk when our research supervisor appeared. Fellow graduate students Greg Farber and Roland Strong were seated at computer terminals, staring at the output from their overnight calculations. After scanning the room, Petsko fixed us with a quick stare and then ordered us to accompany him back to his office. Dutifully, we rose from our workstations and followed him in silence across the hall and back through the main lab. There, two men and one woman stood together in business attire, looking at us expectantly. Without any preamble our boss introduced us and stated that we would be happy to talk to them. He then announced, "guys, our visitors today are from a company called Payload Systems. They're here to speak to you about protein crystallization in space."

We were all quite familiar with the concept of exploiting spaceflight and zero gravity to grow better protein crystals. Crystallization experiments had been flown on various shuttle missions throughout the 1980s with mixed results. Those experiments were on hiatus, waiting for the end of a shutdown that had already extended for over two years following the *Challenger* explosion. The investigators running those experiments had reported the growth of unusually large crystals of several different proteins.

Those experiments, generated by using proteins that were admittedly also extremely easy to crystallize on Earth, had failed on other space flights. At one of the lowest points in the history of space-based protein crystallization, on Shuttle mission STS-51-B in April of 1985, thirty-three out of thirty-four samples failed to crystallize whatsoever, a failure attributed to vibration, shaking, and temperature fluctuations occurring over the duration of the shuttle flight. Nonetheless, NASA was bullish on the technology. One statement from the space agency claimed, "These experiments could improve food production and lead to innovative new drugs to combat cancer, AIDS, high blood pressure, organ transplant rejection, rheumatoid arthritis, and many other diseases." Clearly, the marketing arm of the US space agency had seized on protein crystallography as a possible selling point for the continuation and expansion of space exploration and research.

Most, if not all, of us in the Petsko lab felt that even the most positive of the results reported from the NASA-based experiments were largely uninformative and ambiguous, and that their corresponding claims about prospects of such efforts were overblown. We were well aware of many alternative ways in which crystallization experiments on Earth could be improved via much more straightforward approaches. Even if zero gravity did improve crystallization to some extent, we were skeptical that the cost and effort involved in such an approach would yield new structures, or better structures. A better option would be to simply equip laboratories on Earth, at much lower cost, with the best possible crystallization and X-ray equipment.

As the first descriptions and corresponding hype surrounding NASA's crystallization experiments started to appear in the scientific literature, we read those papers and the resulting commentary and interviews in the press with a combination of interest, amusement, and cynicism. A line in one news article attributed to a prominent academic researcher working with NASA, Dr. Alex McPherson at the University of California, Riverside, drew our particular attention. "Protein crystal growth is a very new area," he stated. "In the past, it was left to students and technicians. Only in the last few years, because of its importance in molecular biology, has it really gotten any attention from scientists."

We quickly decided that such a bold statement could not go unanswered. Without consulting our boss, we composed and mailed a letter:

> Dear Professor McPherson,
>
> It was with great enthusiasm and interest that we read the article in Science News dealing with protein crystal growth. We also feel that protein crystal growth has not been given adequate attention. A number of us are doing our part to remedy this problem. You will be interested to learn about our most recent work involving various additives that affect crystal growth. For instance, we have found that bovine manure and clotted cream have both been extremely beneficial. However, our experiments in which we played Pat Robertson speeches at high volume have had the most deleterious of effects.
>
> But we are not scientists; we are only graduate students. For example, we have not been able to grow lysozyme crystals less than 0.5 mm on a side. Now that eminent scientists like yourself are interested in this problem, we look forward to real progress being made.
>
> Sincerely yours,
>
> Petsko Lab Grad Students.
>
> P.S. Can we send the dead fish to the same address, or would you like it sent to your home?

P.P.S. Where is Riverside, and are there any other eminent scientists there to assist you in your work?

The reply to our missive was swift.

Dear Young Folks,

Thank you for your interesting letter describing your most recent work pertaining to protein crystal growth. I was, of course, not surprised to learn that bovine manure again proved successful in your hands, as it has long been a staple of the research in your laboratory and a major component of its success. I was, however, surprised by your success with rotten milk. Are you quite certain that when you set up your crystal trials none of you were drooling? Perhaps one of you had a runny nose?

With regard to your inquiry as to where Riverside is, it is one of those many places out there in the real world where graduate students go when they leave MIT.

Best wishes for your continued success,

Alexander McPherson

Professor and Chair

Our meeting with the representatives from Payload Systems was pleasant but guarded. The company representatives who had come to Cambridge that morning included one of its co-founders, Anthony Arrott, who had earned a PhD in biomedical engineering from MIT about five years prior, and its managing director, George Economy. The three of us toured the lab with our guests, while they outlined the background of their company.

Payload Systems was based about fifteen miles outside of

Cambridge in Wellesley, where it resided in cramped office space above a hardware store in the town's retail core. The company had been founded in 1984 by Anthony and MIT classmate Byron Lichtenberg, who had earned a PhD in electrical engineering. Lichtenberg, a former US Air Force fighter pilot who flew one hundred thirty-eight combat missions during the Vietnam War, had become a mission specialist for the Shuttle program and had flown a mission on the Shuttle in November of 1983, becoming the first non-government passenger to join a Shuttle crew. Shortly after that flight, during a dinner together at the officers' club at Edwards Air Force Base, the two friends decided to start a company that would work with corporations and governmental agencies wishing to conduct space-based research through NASA. The idea was to serve as the middleman to those organizations and firms that wished to launch payloads into space but lacked the institutional knowledge necessary to work successfully with NASA in a commercial capacity.

Now, four years later, Payload Systems had grown to ten employees and built a client base that included Boeing, Lockheed, MIT, and multiple governments around the world. They had made considerable progress in becoming a significant player in space-based commercial activities but had suddenly seen their sole supplier of microgravity (and with it their entire business model and all their potential contracts and income) shut down by the grounding of the Space Shuttle. They were desperate to identify a new source of zero gravity, as well as to generate a "killer app" that deep-pocketed industrial customers might wish to access—and for which they'd be willing to pay handsomely. Years later, Anthony would tell a science writer at the Fred Hutchinson Cancer Center, "We were looking at that time for what we could do. We didn't know how long it was going to last. We were just trying to save the business."

That morning Anthony did most of the talking on the company's side, asking us in a variety of ways about our opinions on microgravity crystallization, while telling us of their vision of building a business in which they would act as a conduit for pharmaceutical companies to place their protein samples and crystallization experiments into near-earth orbit and microgravity. Roland, Greg, and I didn't mince words; we informed them of the multiple reasons why we felt the concept was flawed. Anthony didn't flinch. As a former MIT grad student, he was familiar with the no-nonsense type of dialogue that dominated the hallways at the Institute, and was in no way put off by our honest responses. He continued to probe and question.

During our conversation, Anthony also addressed the obvious question of how his company intended to get back into the space business. His unexpected answer immediately grabbed our attention. Payload Systems was negotiating a contract with the Soviet space program to place the first American scientific experiments on the *Mir* space station. My initial thought? *That's never going to happen.* My belief was solidly grounded in the reality of geopolitics and the ongoing state of the Cold War. We were in the midst of the final year of President Reagan's second term in office, and Soviet–US relations were still frosty and marked by frequent dustups. The same week as Payload's visit to Cambridge, a US Navy cruiser collided with a Soviet counterpart during a deliberate ship-to-ship confrontation in the Black Sea, intended to test the limits of national maritime boundaries. The encounter, which became known in a rather understated manner as the "Black Sea bumping incident," resulted in diplomatic protests lodged by both countries, but no shots fired in anger.

After a bit more than an hour, our three guests thanked us and headed back to their car. Petsko eventually reappeared in the lab and asked how the visit had gone while simultaneously explaining and apologizing for the lack of warning and preparation for the visit. Our guests had made a prior appointment to talk directly to him, he said, but he had neglected to note it on his calendar and had been both surprised by their appearance that morning and unable to talk to them at length due to a pressing matter elsewhere. We smiled amongst ourselves, being familiar with Greg's lack of careful scheduling and daily habit of dashing from one fire to another. No worries, we assured him. They were an interesting group, but we wouldn't be hearing back from them again. We were sure of it.

> 7 February 1988
> To: Gregory A. Petsko
> Dear Greg,
>
> I would like to thank you and your students for meeting with us on Thursday. The meeting gave us a better understanding of the art of protein crystallography and confirmed our belief that the active participation of crystallographers in the early design and planning phases of the project is essential. We appreciated the participation of Greg, Roland, and Barry. Their thoughtful and articulate responses raised important concerns about performing protein crystal growth in microgravity. Their specific crystallization experiments pose an interesting range of problems and would serve as useful test candidates.
>
> We are interested in discussing your lab's possible involvement with Payload Systems on the project. We would like to meet again to determine your students' level of interest and availability over the next few months. At this meeting, we will describe the entire project in greater detail.
>
> Again, thank you for your assistance. Our time with you, Greg, Roland, and Barry gave us an important appreciation of the concerns and requirements of protein crystallographers. We welcome the opportunity to develop a credible multiple spaceflight program with your assistance.
>
> Sincerely,
> George J. Economy
> Managing Director

When the letter from Payload Systems arrived in our laboratory early the following week, we were astounded. Had we not been clear in expressing our reservations? Who were these guys, anyway?

Despite our skepticism, it took the three of us no more than a single beer at the Muddy Charles that evening to agree to sign up for the project. There were two reasons the decision was easy. The first was scientific—the opportunity to investigate the potential of microgravity for protein crystallization from an unbiased and skeptical perspective seemed important. But for the three of us (all born at the height of the Cold War and raised during the Space Race), there was a more important reason, which Roland summed up perfectly in his office many years later. "If somebody asks you if you want to go to Russia to send experiments into space, you say YES!"

# BUREAUCRATS, RUSSIANS, LAWYERS, AND CONGRESSMEN

February 25, 1988

"It is not in the best interests of this nation to become dependent on foreign entities for our space research."
—Congressman Bill Nelson of Florida

**ONCE WE AGREED** to work with Payload Systems, our responsibilities and workload increased immediately. Seeing that Payload Systems had quickly added the Petsko lab (and our own names) to their advertised roster of "an expert team of crystallographers, engineers, and advisors" for their new research opportunity, we lost no time in making our activities and presence known to our neighbors at MIT. A flyer was generated and posted next to the doorway to our lab, advertising the formation of "Crystals in Space, Ltd: A Subsidiary of Petsko North Inc." Above its prominent tagline (*Better Crystals for a Strong America*), Roland, Greg, and I had respectively listed ourselves as the president, CEO, and chairman of our group.

We were tasked by Payload with the responsibility of designing crystallization problems for an initial set of experiments, and also to work with their engineers to design and test the corresponding hardware for those experiments. Barely two weeks after our first meeting with Payload, the three of us had hardly begun to discuss our ideas when a front-page news story appeared without warning in the Sunday edition of the *New York Times*. The story clearly described the magnitude of the gamble that Payload was taking in conceiving the project, not to mention entrusting three young graduate students to design and carry out the experiments:

> American Company and Soviets Agree on Space Venture
> First Commercial Pact
> Plan for Experiments in Orbit Comes after Delay in U.S. Satellite Launchings
> By William J. Broad
> February 21, 1988.
>
> For the first time an American company has contracted to have the Soviet Union carry Western commercial payloads into orbit. The agreement is likely to spur similar moves by other companies, Federal officials said. The plan is an indication of the eagerness of private companies to perform commercial research in space despite the two-year grounding of the American space shuttles. It also marks one of the biggest successes to date in the Soviet drive to market the Russian space program, which was once shrouded in secrecy. Now and for the immediate future, the Soviet Union has an advantage over the West in conducting some long-duration experiments in space because of its orbiting Mir space station.

The article went on to quote anonymous officials in the US Department of Commerce who described and defended their approval of the program. They argued that American corporations needed access to space, and that since such access would not be forthcoming on American rockets and platforms in the near future, the Russians should be viewed as a valid alternative for American industry. Pushing back against the concern that important scientific secrets might be inadvertently handed over to the Soviet Union, a lawyer who had helped draft the export license application at the Commerce Department was quoted as stating that there was "no chance sensitive technologies would fall into Russian hands . . . . It's different from the usual perceived risks of technology transfer; this is a situation where we are keeping America from falling behind technologically."

The article concluded with a bold statement that proved to be prescient for many years afterwards: "In the wake of the *Mir* agreement, some Western experts have speculated that the government's position is softening and that future export licenses might be granted for American satellites to fly atop Russian rockets."

The company's contract with the Soviet space agency and the corresponding export license, which were both issued by the US Department of Commerce, had been quietly and secretly negotiated by Payload Systems over the past year. According to Jeffrey Manber, who worked at the time in the Commerce Department's Office of Space Commerce (and who later described the process in his memoir *Selling Peace*), getting the necessary US government approvals was a delicate and closely guarded process. The application and subsequent review and approval process were coordinated between the Departments of Commerce and Defense, while being kept secret from the State Department, NASA, and Congress, who were each largely and vocally opposed to US collaboration with the Soviet space program. Members and employees of each, along with the US government at-large and the rest of the nation, learned of the deal and its governmental approval at the same time as the three graduate students who comprised Payload's expert team of crystallographers— by reading about it in the *New York Times* over their coffee and donuts that Sunday morning.

Additional news outlets around the country and the world quickly repeated and built upon the initial news story. Within days, a "shocked" Florida congressman Bill Nelson (who had flown on the final Shuttle mission before the *Challenger* disaster, and in so doing had bumped Greg Jarvis into the doomed flight crew of the subsequent ill-fated mission) threatened to "do everything we can to prevent the experiment from flying." A follow-up story in the *New York Times*, also written by William Broad, was published five days after the announcement of the project:

> HOUSE PANEL CHIEF QUESTIONS PACT WITH RUSSIANS ON SPACE PAYLOAD
>
> The chairman of a House subcommittee criticized the Commerce Department yesterday for granting an export license to an American company that has contracted to fly commercial payloads aboard a Soviet space station. The chairman, Representative Bill Nelson, Democrat of Florida, heads the House Science and Technology Subcommittee on Space Science and Applications. He said the decision-making process was questionable and set a bad precedent, and he said he would call a hearing on the matter. His district includes the Kennedy Space Center . . . . David Dickerson, an aide to Mr. Nelson, said that if the hearing, in April or May, failed to clear up questions, "We will do everything we can to prevent the experiment from flying."

The article went on to describe how Payload Systems had ignited a turf war within the government, with the State Department and the Florida congressman charging the Commerce Department with bypassing the government's International Traffic in Arms regulations. The Commerce Department promptly responded that its actions "were totally appropriate within those regulations," pointedly adding, "There is no military sensitivity here. Even the Defense Department has no objection."

That a private company could manage to build a business model based on doing business in space in partnership with the Soviet space program was facilitated by a recent change in philosophy within the federal government driven by the Reagan administration. Since the early 1980s, it had encouraged the growth of free-market initiatives, including space-based commerce that might be underwritten and supported by organizations other than NASA. While NASA had positioned itself as the gatekeeper to space and zero gravity, the bureaucracy, red tape, and inertia within its walls had discouraged companies from making serious efforts to pursue research efforts in space. The *Challenger* disaster and subsequent loss of Shuttle service had served as the final nail in the coffin of many corporations' space research departments; those that persisted were clearly in the market for reliable access to zero gravity, wherever that access might be found.

The deal struck between Payload, the Soviet space program, and the US Department of Commerce was the product of a perfect storm of political and economic change in the US and the USSR. The rise to power of Mikhail Gorbachev several years earlier had been accompanied by *perestroika* ("restructuring") of the Soviet model of centralized economic planning across all sectors of the USSR, including an edict that government programs should strive to generate commercial contracts and funding, fostering partnerships that extended to other governments and private industry around the world.

The subsequent creation of Glavkosmos (the governmental agency in charge of commercialization of the Soviet space exploration program) in February of 1985 had preceded the grounding of the US Shuttle program by only eleven months. Into the void left by the absence of the American space program, and onward through the door cracked open by almost simultaneous social and political change in the Soviet Union, strolled Payload Systems and Anthony Arrott.

Arrott and his colleagues had cold-called the Soviet embassy in

Washington, DC, and inquired if Glavkosmos would be interested in contracting with Payload Systems to place pharmaceutical experiments onto their space station. Furthermore, would they be open to negotiating a secret contract spelling out a set price and clear payment terms, and would they be willing to commit to time and training of cosmonauts to install, operate, and return experimental hardware as part of a flight mission?

Would they agree to remain blind to the nature of the experiments, and to hold all aspects of their operation and outcome entirely confidential?

Would they allow all intellectual property rights to remain with the customer?

Would they allow the experiments to remain aboard the space station for up to two months?

The answer to each question was an emphatic *yes*.

The drafting of the application for an export license, which ultimately needed to be approved by the Secretary of the Department of Commerce, was fraught with political maneuvering that is common inside the beltway of our nation's capital. Knowing full well that even the slightest whiff by NASA of a government-sanctioned deal between an American firm and the Soviet space agency would mean immediate resistance by that department, officials in the Commerce Department's space program (including Jeff, who would eventually join the Payload Systems team in Moscow as part of an official observation group for the first mission) quietly enlisted the support and approval of representatives of the Department of Defense and Commerce's own Export Control administration.

A lawyer from the DC firm of Hogan & Hartson (Ann Flowers, who would also join us in Moscow) prepared the text of the export license application, drawing heavily upon the terms of the proposed contract between Payload Systems and the Soviets. Unbeknownst to their newly hired team of graduate students, a key feature of that contract, termed "zero technology transfer," would dictate how our own work would proceed over the next year. Simply put, the experiments and the hardware would have to be designed in a manner that allowed the Russians to activate and deactivate them without gaining any knowledge of their exact composition or inner workings. The three of us were tasked, in collaboration with Payload engineers, to create simple black boxes containing the experiments. Their operation would consist of the simple turning of exposed screws. In return, the Soviets would expect only that we would provide a generic listing of the types of compounds and materials within the devices and a guarantee of their non-hazardous nature— with no description of their exact composition.

The final version of the application detailed how the project would benefit American commerce and industry without transferring new technological knowledge to the Soviet Union, and without running afoul of the federal government's "Munition List"—US goods and services that were strictly prohibited from being exported to the Soviet Union. In a final effort to avoid the attention of NASA, the wording of the final draft of the application vaguely requested a license to "conduct industrial research in a Soviet laboratory."

The somewhat important detail that the laboratory in question was actually located on the *Mir* space station was buried deep inside the text of the application.

The export license, providing the necessary governmental approval for Payload Systems to fly experiments on the Russian space station, was quietly approved over the first six weeks of 1988, starting with review by the Department of Defense's export bureau and then by the Commerce Department.

Incredibly, the first-ever commercial deal between an American company and the Soviet space agency was discussed and approved by two different agencies within the US government without a single outside federal official, politician, or reporter (other than one William J. Broad, who had been previously invited to write an exclusive about the project for the *New York Times*) having heard a single word about it.

# PROTEINS, PLASTICS, GREASE, AND GASKETS

## December 1988

"One more pothole will be the end of me."

**I WAS SITTING** in the passenger seat of a road-worn Boston sedan driven by an engineer from Payload Systems. His car was held together by not much more than corrosion and faith. My driver and companion that morning, Bob Renshaw, was chauffeuring the two of us and the latest prototypes of our crystallization devices to a testing laboratory in the Boston suburbs. There they would be subjected to various forces of acceleration, vibration, and depressurization as part of flight certification for eventual deployment on the *Mir* space station. The hardware, loaded with chemical solutions intended to mimic the protein samples and crystallization reagents that it would eventually hold, was encased in sheets of pH-sensitive indicator paper that would dramatically change color if the contents were to leak at any point in the testing process.

The results of the examination would be summarily described in a subsequent report that would be disseminated to both the company's leadership and to the Soviets. We were working on a tight schedule for the successful design and production of flight hardware that could pass inspection and be approved for use on *Mir*, and our margin for error was growing thinner by the day.

Bob's car was apparently devoid of any form of meaningful shock absorption. Every encounter with a rough patch in the road transmitted to my internal organs with a jolt that exacerbated an already delicate physical situation. The night before, I had attended a celebration to commemorate a successful thesis defense by one of my classmates. The evening had progressed as such occasions tend to do until I had caught the final train back to my apartment in a significant alcoholic haze. Fortunately, the presence of well-liquored college students on the MBTA at 12:30 a.m. was not at all uncommon, particularly on the Red Line that connected Tufts, Harvard, MIT, and Boston University. I had stumbled off the train at my designated stop near Symphony Hall and wandered to my apartment without encountering friend or foe.

Such a conclusion to an evening out was now almost unheard of for me. Shortly before the end of my first semester at the Institute, I had met a Midwestern transplant to the Boston area named Amy. Within several months, our friendship evolved into an unexpected relationship (cemented in my imagination by an afternoon together watching the Red Sox at Fenway Park, for which she never paid me back the price of her ticket). We had now been married for a few months, meaning I had a wife to whom I would have to present and explain myself in our apartment on the third floor of our brownstone walk-up.

Now it was early the next day, and I was being repeatedly slammed up and down as we cruised the surface streets of the Boston suburbs. I had met Bob that morning at the new company headquarters in Cambridge. Payload Systems had recently moved from Wellesley to newly rented office space near MIT, about three blocks down Third Street from Kendall Square. It was a great move for our project; we could now join their staff for meetings after a short stroll across the Institute campus and down the street.

The only downside to the new location was the neighborhood, which was slowly emerging from an extended period of urban decay and was still prone to occasional street crime. Shortly after their move, an engineer working late at night had been startled by the sound of shattering glass at the front of their space. Dashing into the lobby from his office, he had encountered an intruder making off with a new fax machine. After chasing the intruder into the street, the engineer was quickly halted in his pursuit when the burglar hurled the machine at him and then dashed off into the night.

Bob was aware of my discomfort over the course of our drive and clearly enjoying every moment of it. A short, bearded Englishman with a gleam in his eye and an appearance not unlike a satyr (although without the hind legs of a horse), he was a man of considerable intelligence, joviality, and off-color humor that I normally enjoyed greatly. This morning, however, I needed gentle treatment that was not forthcoming.

The prototype flight hardware that I was holding in my lap that morning was the product of designs that Roland, Greg, and I had suggested and sketched out, that were intended to satisfy the requirement of three s's: secrecy, simplicity, and safety. The export license approved earlier in the year by the US Commerce Department mandated that the Russians be kept in the dark regarding the identity of the molecules, the ingredients of the experiments, and the internal workings of the hardware. Our own desire was that the experiments be virtually impossible to screw up; nothing more than a few simple turns of a knob would start and stop each crystallization trial. And of course, neither the equipment nor its contents could pose a hazard to the health and safety of the cosmonauts who would share their living space with our devices for upwards of two to three months.

We had quickly decided to test two different hardware designs, to increase the possibility that we would see a significant improvement in crystal growth in zero gravity. The first design simply replicated the usual type of crystallization experiment set up on Earth, in which the slow evaporation of water from each protein drop (and capture of that water vapor in adjacent sealed reservoirs inside the device) would hopefully result in protein crystallization. This technique was termed "Vapour Diffusion," and the device that we intended to design and use on the space station was simply referred to as a "VD."

In the second design, two neighboring solutions (protein in one; a crystallization agent in the other) would initially be separated by a physical boundary. That barrier would be opened in orbit, leading to slow mixing of the solutions and crystallization of the protein. While such an approach could not easily be employed on Earth (because the two solutions and their molecules would mix together too rapidly), in zero gravity the strategy was possible. This alternative technique was termed "Boundary Layer Diffusion" and the second device in which it would happen was referred to as a "BLD." Before finally being deemed ready to fly, that piece of hardware would produce enormous anxiety as we struggled with its performance.

It had not been difficult to create an initial design for each of the devices; simple sketches of the basic geometry and dimensions and parts for each one had readily been converted by Payload engineers into manufacturing blueprints. Payload had then engaged the services of student-run machine shops at the Wentworth Institute of Technology in Boston to produce prototypes of the devices. Wentworth had been founded in 1904, through the donation of the estate of businessman Arioch Wentworth for the founding of an industrial engineering school. The campus had been built in the Fenway neighborhood (not far from Amy's and my apartment) where it occupied fifteen buildings and enrolled roughly three thousand students. Unlike many universities, Wentworth placed considerable emphasis on hands-on industrial design and fabrication experience for their students.

As I had learned during the past year, Payload Systems had been overly optimistic regarding potential involvement and funding for their first mission to *Mir* by pharmaceutical companies. A few weeks earlier, Anthony asked me to join him on a trip to one such company in New Jersey to meet with members of its structural biology and drug design research groups. The plan was to talk about the project and promote the possibility of corporate involvement. That afternoon, our presentation had been received courteously and with obvious interest. Finally, Anthony had cut to the chase, asking the gathered investigators whether they felt such an opportunity would be of interest to their groups.

One of the research heads had asked the obvious question. How much would it cost? The answer corresponded to a low six-figure sum. Glancing at his colleagues, he smiled gently at us, and then responded, "Well, I think my signing authority is capped at about six hundred bucks."

Therefore, Payload's first mission would be entirely funded directly from its company coffers. That, in turn, would lead to occasional parsimony that was entirely understandable. Where money needed to be spent, Payload would do so without question, but where money could be saved, they would do so as well.

The most obvious potential for savings that affected our immediate activities and responsibilities was in the design and fabrication of the devices themselves. Rather than hiring an expensive manufacturing company to fabricate the units using injection molding (that could generate intact devices with a minimum number of possible leak points), they instead contracted the fabrication process to an academic institution manned by students, and then committed to designs for the devices that relied on less expensive machining and assembly from individual slabs of plastic. The individual pieces of the devices would then be screwed together with grease and rubber gaskets in between the various solid components, in hopes of preventing leakage of the fluids held inside.

The issue of maintaining both internal seals in the devices (to prevent cross-contamination between individual solutions) and external seals (to prevent the same solutions from escaping into the environment of the *Mir* space station) would consume much of my attention for several stress-filled months. Because the units would eventually be assembled on-site in Kazakhstan by the investigators (from individual parts that were to be fabricated and delivered by Wentworth), there was considerable opportunity for variation in their performance. A single flawed gasket or seal, or a single attachment point screwed together too loosely or too tightly, invited leakage.

Our first test of a device prototype in the company lab was memorable. We had assembled and loaded the device with colored salt solutions, sealed it, wrapped it in indicator paper, and placed it into a vacuum bell jar. Slowly and carefully, we started to evacuate the chamber by pulling an external vacuum. We needed to get down to approximately 10 percent of atmospheric pressure and hold for ten minutes without leakage.

Instead, within a second or two (and with only a mild vacuum being pulled) the device violently regurgitated its liquid contents from multiple points, not only staining the indicator paper but tearing it apart. Liquid droplets and pieces of paper coated the inside of the vacuum chamber as if it were the site of a violent murder.

We spent the following weeks refining both the design of the hardware and the protocols corresponding to their assembly. The weak link in their performance was clearly in the precision with which the sealing gaskets were machined and then placed as the devices were put together. Particularly for the BLD units, the seals between its single moving part (a rotating partition that would be turned by 90 degrees to expose the two solutions to one another) and the flanking chambers was giving us plenty of trouble and frustration. Whereas we had been able to certify the reliability of the VD devices after a few tries, the BLD units proved continually troublesome. On one occasion, a device had leaked while being subjected to nothing other than the banging, jolts, and vibrations associated with a ride in Bob's car, and thus arrived at the testing facility having already visibly failed. We turned around and drove back to Cambridge in silence, the flames of Bob's fiery personality temporarily quenched.

By the time 1988 was drawing to a close, we had produced a version of a BLD unit, incorporating several design changes, that appeared to hold its water in our preliminary in-house tests (including my own primitive approach of violently shaking a filled device in one hand while cursing at it under my breath). We had scheduled an official certification test on a cold December morning, and I endured the most uncomfortable ride yet to the facility in hungover silence.

We were met by a technician who greeted us with a smile. He had witnessed our prior failures and was deeply sympathetic and supportive. I was not only on pins and needles from the prior night's celebration and subsequent car ride, I was also quite anxious. We were exactly one year away from our scheduled first mission, and in that year there would be much that still needed to be accomplished. Among them: yet another round of certification and operation of our prototypes in an actual zero-gravity simulation; subsequent fabrication of the actual devices to be placed into orbit; final face-to-face meetings with our Russian counterparts to provide documentation of device performance and precise protocols for their handling and operation; and finally ground-based crystallization trials in copies of the flight hardware. There was little or no time left for another design iteration; an order for fabrication of actual flight hardware needed to be placed soon. Another certification failure would probably result in the abandonment of the BLD design, half of our proposed experiments, and a corresponding waste of Payload's money that had been spent developing the device.

After an hour, Bob and I emerged from the facility smiling, with the hardware back in its cases, test results in his briefcase. My malaise had lifted, and the day was suddenly bright and cheery. The final version of the BLD had passed every test. We were back on course and ready to enter a final year's sprint towards Moscow, Kazakhstan, and crystals in space.

# ZERO G-FECTS

"The Society of Interplanetary Free Floaters hereby extends honorary membership to Barry Stoddard. Said membership is the direct consequence of this individual's gross and flagrant violation of the irrevocable law of gravity while participating in aerial flight as diagrammed above. For durations of up to thirty million micro-seconds, weightlessness and the accompanying mayhem prevailed within the test aircraft as our new member strove to master his environment. Unlike a seasoned astronaut, the free-floater distinguished himself by demonstrating a tendency toward gastronomic upheaval, and in future "bull sessions" he is encouraged to disseminate an accurate bag-by-bag account of the aforementioned traumatic experience."
—NASA Certificate of Interplanetary Free Floaters.

March 1, 1989

**IT WAS A** beautiful Wednesday morning in Texas. I had flown down to Houston the night before to test our crystallization hardware in a zero-gravity environment. To do that, I would be spending two days on jet flights run by NASA out of Ellington Field, which produced short, repeated periods of weightlessness. Those periods of zero gravity were produced by a roller-coaster in the sky traveling at speeds up to almost seven hundred miles per hour aboard a KC-135 jet flying at 35,000 feet being flown through repeated violent ascents and descents. As the jet flew over the top of each ascent, the contents and individual in the belly of the aircraft would float within their designated area of the cabin. Conversely, at the bottom of each descent, the same contents and people were pressed into the floor at twice the normal gravitational force. The entire process lasted for about three straight hours and was informally referred to by the flight staff and crew as a "bounce flight." For many first-time passengers, the plane—and the experience within—became known as the "Vomit Comet."

The purpose of this trip was to satisfy a final requirement stated in Payload's contract with the Soviet space program—that all flight hardware be safety- and performance-tested in a zero-gravity environment, as part of the lengthy process to eventually send our equipment into orbit.

With this requirement in mind, the goals of my trip were twofold: first, to demonstrate that the equipment could be operated according to a simple protocol while in a weightless condition, and second, to demonstrate that the same equipment would not display a failure in zero gravity. The first issue was straightforward—the only thing an astronaut would be asked to do is to turn a few knobs on each device once or twice. The second issue was a bit more questionable; the depressing tendency of our hardware to leak their contents, although now appearing to be solved, still weighed on my mind. Whereas on Earth that leak might amount to a bit of fluid dripping innocuously down the side of the apparatus, on the space station the possibility of experimental liquids floating around and eventually ending up inside an electrical control panel (or worse yet, an astronaut's mouth or eye) was something nobody wanted to imagine (hence the additional requirement for documented quality-control testing in zero gravity).

Before the hardware or I would be allowed anywhere near a NASA bounce flight, I had been required to submit myself to a physical exam conducted by a military physician, and then to attend a one-day training course run by the Navy to become educated on the physiological effects of spatial disorientation brought on by rapid changes in G-forces. The doctor's exam had been taken care of a few months earlier on a crisp September afternoon in Boston and proved to be no problem, as I was in my mid-twenties and in decent physical shape. The doctor did note that I was substantially red-green colorblind and produced a certificate that approved me for further "physiological training" by the United States military, but banned me from using color signals to land my fighter plane on the deck of an aircraft carrier. I informed him that would not pose a problem.

Several weeks later in late October, I found myself in a large lecture hall at a Navy air station in Corpus Christi, surrounded by future aircrew who were similarly required to become informed on the nature of disorientation and discomfort that might accompany high-speed flight conditions. They regarded the short, somewhat long-haired graduate student dressed in a Hawaiian shirt and jeans sitting in their midst with mild interest, but asked no questions. Armed with a folder containing my own Flight Personnel Training Qualification Forms, I settled into a seat and waited for class instruction to start. I was scheduled to participate in two exercises— visual and disorientation training, followed by altitude, air compression, and oxygen tolerance training in the afternoon. I was disappointed to see that I would not be participating in subsequent exercises on day two that covered "explosive decompression," "submarine escape and diving," and "centrifuge and ejection seats."

The lecture, delivered by a tall, soft-spoken officer, was straightforward. He described the effects of disconnection between real and perceived motion and spatial disorientation. His point was clear—everyone in a cockpit might easily succumb to the effects of motion sickness, military pilots included. However, anyone hoping to fly jets for our country would have to successfully adapt strategies that kept the problem manageable while flying a wildly expensive and extremely complicated aircraft.

The hour-long lecture systematically described symptoms, behavioral methods to minimize them, and allowable medicinal strategies for would-be pilots. At its conclusion, the aircrew candidates (and one increasingly nervous graduate student) were informed that they would now complete the morning's session by a quick assessment of their own brain's susceptibility and reaction to spatial and inertial disorientation. Expecting that we would be led into a big room and strapped into high-tech flight simulator, I was surprised to see a pair of service crew carry out what looked like a bar stool to the middle of the lecture stage. At once, the atmosphere in the room became subdued. Clearly a significant test of courage, strength, and fortitude was at hand.

The instructor gazed into the crowd with the intent of choosing the first individual for a demonstration. As I slid deeper into my seat, his eyes locked onto me, and then he requested that "Jimmy Buffett" join him front and center. After a moment's hesitation, I stood. The other attendees looked at me, and then began to chuckle and whisper amongst themselves. *This*, they were thinking, *should be entertaining*. I squeezed out of my row, walked to the stage, and stopped obediently by the chair, which really was a large leather bar stool that had clearly seen many years of hard use. I was asked for my course paperwork and told to remove my watch and sit in the chair; I was then instructed to make a fist on my left thigh, bend over, put the side of my head on the top of the fist, and close my eyes.

"You're going to be spun rapidly for fifteen seconds," the instructor informed me cordially. "When that stops, please stand up from the chair as quickly as you can."

I felt hands on the chair and my shoulders, and I was then spinning in tight little circles—slowly at first, then with increasing speed. *This is easy!* I thought. I had expected that "physiological training" would involve being strapped into an expensive and complex machine and tested as if I were an astronaut-in-training. Instead, I was being spun around as if I were attending a five-year-old's birthday party.

The chair stopped abruptly. "STAND UP! HURRY!" yelled the suddenly much less congenial instructor. I opened my eyes and sat up confidently with the intention of jumping from the chair. However, my body's uncoiling proved to be difficult to stop; with surprising speed, my torso and head lurched violently backwards and counterclockwise, toppling me unceremoniously out of the chair. Aghast and somewhat stunned, I lurched to my feet, only to immediately fall to the floor again.

The effect on the room was electric, but the attendees were supportive. Rather than uncontrollable laughter and mockery, the group of young men were shouting encouragingly and happily. Finally staggering to an upright position (although with the room still spinning), I steadied myself uncertainly. The instructor was now gently smiling.

"Would you like to try again, Jimmy?"

"Ummm . . . not unless it's absolutely required."

"Okay, I think we can give you a conditional pass on this. Just don't plan on ever flying jets for the United States Navy."

After the morning's drama, the afternoon's session (on decompression and the effect of oxygen deprivation that might accompany the loss of air pressure in a cockpit at high altitude) proved much more straightforward. Placed into a sealed chamber in groups of eight to ten individuals at a time, pairs of us were tasked with challenging one another with flash cards displaying simple mathematical problems while the chamber was slowly decompressed, and the atmospheric oxygen content reduced. The idea was to have the pilot candidates experience and recognize the disorientation and loss of cognitive abilities that would accompany the loss of oxygen pressure.

In practice, the largest challenge during our time together in the decompression chamber that afternoon was the extensive amount of flatulence that broke out among the group of individuals sitting close together in the sealed chamber.

The trip to Ellington Field and NASA had gotten off to a challenging start almost immediately. Upon landing at Houston Intercontinental Airport and presenting myself at the rental car counter, I discovered that my driver's license was missing in action. The previous night had marked my first birthday since getting married the prior summer; Amy and I had splurged on a dinner out to celebrate. As always, my ID had been checked for proof of legal drinking age (a frequent occurrence in those days, since I barely looked as if I might be old enough to attend my junior prom). Rather than put my license back into my wallet, I had instead pushed it into my jacket pocket and forgotten to retrieve it. In the late 1980s, you could easily board and take a commercial airline flight without showing a license or any other form of identification, but you couldn't rent a car upon arrival at your designation. And so, a nearly forty-mile taxi ride later, I had checked into a cheap hotel outside of Ellington Field Joint Military Base in Clear Lake Texas. The staff informed me that they could transport me to and from the entry gate of the facility for the activities that awaited me over the next two days.

Originally built in 1917 a few miles south of Houston, Ellington Field was constructed for flight training as part of the US entry into World War I. Its early years of service were marked by frantic war-time training activities (including education of bomber crews and WACs during World War II and Air Force crews during the subsequent Cold War) bracketed by periods of far less activity. From the 1950s through the '70s, Ellington Field provided training for aircrews in multiple active and reserve branches of the military.

In the 1960s, NASA created its own facilities for astronaut training at Ellington, capitalizing on its proximity to the new Manned Spacecraft Center (eventually known to the world as "Mission Control") less than ten miles away.

Wednesday morning dawned bright and warm. After enjoying a heavy hotel breakfast, which would soon prove to be a highly regrettable mistake, I was driven to the facility by a hotel employee, with flight hardware safely stowed in a cheap plastic toolbox purchased specifically for zero-gravity testing. I had been up late the previous night loading the same salt solutions and indicator dyes into chambers of each unit, and then taping strips of indicator paper along each surface and seam of the devices at points where leakage might occur.

I had been worried that my lack of government-issued ID might be problematic for gaining entrance to the facility, but my concerns proved moot. The paperwork that I had been provided by Payload Systems, indicating that I had a reservation on the morning's bounce flight, along with my FAA-issued Medical Certificate Second Class and a hard-won Naval flight operations training qualification form (signed by a Lieutenant "G. Wavell" on that fateful morning in Corpus Christi), was sufficient for me to be waved through the security gate by a bored-looking serviceman. I walked into a large two-story building and entered the front door. In a cramped room filled with folding chairs, a diverse group of individuals found their seats.

A pair of female NASA technicians wearing brilliant blue jumpsuits with large American flag patches on their shoulders entered the room and stood in front of us. Smiling brightly, they welcomed us to the day's zero-gravity bounce flight and introduced themselves. We were informed that five separate groups, ranging in size from a single individual sent from a company in Cambridge, to a team of investigators from a medical research program in an unnamed neighboring country to the north, would be on the flight. Each team would be assigned a section of the KC-135 cabin to conduct necessary assessments of their hardware and standard operating procedures. Large equipment was already onboard; smaller devices such as mine would be hand-carried by their respective owners onto the plane and remain with them through the duration of the flight.

The entire flight from departure to landing would last slightly less than three hours, including a series of roughly forty parabolic ascents and descents, each producing a thirty-second period of weightlessness at the top, followed by its doubled G-force counterpart at the bottom of each cycle. We were informed that during takeoff, we would all be seated in a few rows of seats in the very rear of the aircraft, and then (upon achieving "bounce-flight" altitude of 35,000 feet) would have several minutes to make our way to our designated test area.

The technicians then became more serious. "As you know, parabolic flight parameters can produce significant motion-related distress and nausea, particularly for those who have never flown with us before. If you're new to zero-gravity bounce flights, we suggest that you consider riding out the first few cycles while still belted into your seat, before you move into the open cabin. And above all else, *do not* neglect to use and then properly seal your waste bags if you get sick. The pilots *will not* stop the flight if particles of vomit are floating through the aircraft. They will simply close and seal the cockpit door."

The room became hushed as everyone considered the depressing scenario that the flight technician had just described. I had been preceded by Roland in this activity, who had traveled to Texas and carried out a first round of tests of the hardware a couple months earlier. His graphic description of the completely debilitating motion sickness he experienced was sobering. I vowed that under no circumstances would I embarrass myself or Payload Systems.

Standing, I filed out of the room and followed the men in the group into a small changing area where bundles of grey military flight suit awaited us, all far less fashionable than those worn by the NASA technicians. I quickly changed into mine, and, as I viewed my reflection in the mirror, immediately began to hear the soundtrack from the recently released movie *Top Gun* in my head. *Oh yeah,* I thought. *I feel the need for speed!* Memories of my previous unfortunate encounter with the bar stool in Corpus Christi were promptly forgotten.

As we walked to the plane (painted a striking pattern of grey, blue, and white that was reminiscent of Air Force One, with "NASA 930" prominently displayed on the tail), I noted a diagram of a single ascent and descent painted on the fuselage directly below the cockpit. In the diagram, the plane was bending like a dolphin at the top and the bottom of its trajectory, a depiction that I hoped reflected artistic license and imagination. I climbed up the stairs, entered the cabin, and found my way to the seats in the rear of the aircraft.

The take-off was noteworthy for its acceleration and abrupt climb. In a matter of a few minutes, we were leveled off at cruising altitude. One of the technicians stood, faced us, and told us were free to move about the cabin. The first three parabolas, she said, would start in ten minutes, followed by a short break, and then the remaining arcs in succession over the following two hours. The break would allow those who were still seated to join the larger group, and those who were already in the cabin to make any adjustments to their testing plans that might be necessary based on the timing and outcome of their first moments of zero gravity.

Most of the group unbuckled and moved forward to the cabin. I had decided to take the advice offered in the pre-flight briefing and to calmly enjoy my initial zero-gravity experience from the comfort and safety of my seat at the far rear of the plane. Looking forward, I saw people separating into groups distributed over the length of the plane cabin, including one large group that had donned surgical masks and scrubs over their flight suits and appeared to be clustering around a life-sized mannequin strapped to an operating table. *Are they going to . . . practice surgical procedures in zero gravity?* I wondered. And at that moment, the plane suddenly lurched upward at an appalling angle of ascent, its engines roaring.

A minute later and just as suddenly, the nose of the plane began to violently roll over and downward, as it navigated the top arc of its first circuit. I briefly noticed the small sampling of humanity in front of me rise smoothly off the floor, and felt my own body try to similarly rise upwards against my seatbelt. My initial observations of the feeling and effect of simulated weightlessness were abruptly cut short with an overwhelming realization that I was going to vomit within the next few seconds, and not as a preliminary warmup. This was going to be the mother of all stomach upheavals right out of the starting gate.

Frantically, I pulled a NASA-approved vomit bag from a flight suit pocket. Fortunately, the technicians had been very clear during their briefing; everyone should have multiple bags on their person, with the first one fully open and at-the-ready. As well, everyone had been instructed to conduct a dry run with their bags, like a gunslinger in the old West practicing his quick-draw technique. With a single desperate motion, I pulled the bag tightly over my mouth, and my hotel breakfast departed my stomach considerably more rapidly than it had entered earlier in the morning. I quickly sealed it lest my partially digested pancakes, sausage, and eggs join the surgery in progress.

The KC-135 had now gone over the hump and hurtling downhill at nearly the speed of sound, pushing my internal organs up towards my spine. Those in the cabin had descended back to the floor, in most cases moderately close to their starting positions. Just as suddenly, the nose of the plane began to pull up every bit as violently as it had turned downward at the top of the flight pattern, and I was pressed into the bottom and back of my seat with an amount of force that felt far greater than the advertised double-strength gravitational pull.

This half of the plane's acrobatics was even more physically upsetting than the top of the arc. My stomach, already fairly empty, clenched around itself tightly somewhere deep in my torso and began to hunt for any remaining contents to expel. Thirty seconds later, we had exited the bottom of the maneuver and were again hurtling skyward, engines screaming. *This really isn't good for you,* a small voice inside me said. Before I could wholeheartedly agree, the next flip-flop had begun, and again my digestive system attempted to relocate itself to a new site somewhere outside of my skin.

After three circuits, the plane's gyrations momentarily paused. I leaned back in my seat, mouth hanging open, bag clenched shut in my hand, eyes closed.

"I'll take that for you. Are you okay?"

I opened my eyes and registered the smiling face of one of the NASA technicians. I noted in a matter-of-fact way as she removed the bag from my hand that she was quite pretty.

"Ummm . . . yeah, I think I'll be OK. Does it get better as it goes on?"

"Oh no . . . generally if you get sick, you just keep doing it until the end."

I pondered this sad piece of information for a few seconds.

"I think maybe I should just stay back here and try to test my hardware from my seat. What do you think?"

"Yeah, that sounds like a plan. You got your next bag ready?"

Memories of the rest of the flight are mercifully dim, except for vague recollections of feeling every bit as sick, through every single flight cycle over the next hour and a half, as I did on the first one. However, I did manage (through recurring cycles of zero gravity followed each and every time by an equivalent amount of far too much gravity) to drag my little plastic toolbox out from under the seat in front of me, where I had managed to hold onto it between my feet. Removing individual components of the crystallization hardware, I activated and then de-activated each chamber between dry heaves, turning knobs and screws according to my faithfully memorized protocol. Thankfully, the filter paper taped to the equipment surfaces remained dry and unstained.

*Bless you, Wentworth*, I thought during a lucid moment between my repeated bouts of suffering. *I really couldn't endure these things pissing all over themselves right now.*

Immediately upon the completion of the final cycle, normalcy returned to the plane cabin and to my outlook on life. Surprisingly, I even felt hungry. As my fellow travelers returned to their seats for landing, I examined their faces for signs of the fun that I had missed. The range of their visible emotions was wide and obvious. Some were obviously giddy. Others looked as shattered as I had felt until a few minutes earlier. I noted that more than a few flight suit pockets were missing their bags.

Upon landing, I quietly collected my flight hardware and shuffled off the plane. Glancing at the surgical dummy as I walked past him, I noted that bits of vomit were stuck to his exposed chest. *They might want to work on that part of their protocol*, I thought.

The flight crew, all smiles, joined us in the staging area as we changed out of our flight suits and informed us that we were invited to come to lunch across the highway at a lunch spot known as Pe-Te's. My ears pricked up. While I had been physically destroyed by the events of the morning, I was feeling much better now, and as always, I was more than interested in a chance to sample new food.

Located across State Route 3 from Ellington Field, Pe-Te's was a Cajun BBQ joint and dance hall covering seven thousand square feet, created by a son of Louisiana sharecroppers named Les Johnson. Standing all of five foot five inches tall, Les had built and opened Pe-Te's at the site of a former gas station in 1980, after many years of serving BBQ from a truck in a parking lot at Ellington Field to pilots, flight staff, and astronauts in training. The name of the restaurant was an acknowledgment of the owner's small stature. "Pe-Te" was a Cajunized version of the French word *petit*. Over the next twenty-five years until its closing, it served as a site where those who survived a trip on the Vomit Comet would fill their bellies with

Tex-Mex cuisine, all while listening to Cajun and zydeco music and recounting their recent adventure on the bounce flight. The roof and walls were decorated with license plates from around the world and autographed photographs of astronauts who had spent their time and money there. Some of those astronauts had taken tapes of Les Johnson's Saturday morning Cajun radio show with them into space.

Satisfied with a plate of brisket and sides (and amazed that my system was content to take it in), I spent the rest of the day relaxing at the hotel pool under a bright Texas sun, deciding on my course of action for the next day. I was scheduled to repeat the entire events of the morning with a duplicate set of hardware to generate data on its performance from two separate days of bounce flights. For obvious reasons, my enthusiasm for the second session was not high. Later that evening, after documenting the hardware's performance from earlier in the day (while simultaneously deciding to not fully document the performance of the investigator), I loaded the second set of crystallization hardware and arrived at the decision to surrender my fate to NASA and the space gods. *If I puke my guts out again tomorrow,* I thought, *I'm going to do it like an astronaut.*

Day two was every bit as warm and beautiful as day one. Walking to the jet in a fresh flight suit, I had nothing new in my stomach (having more wisely opted to skip the hotel's breakfast offerings) and no lingering questions in my mind. This time, I knew exactly what was ahead of me.

As soon as the plane was at cruising altitude, I unbuckled and made my way to my small bit of officially taped-off space in the cabin. I saw the same NASA technician who had commiserated with me the day before calmly observe me without a trace of reservation or apprehension. *Nothing she hasn't seen before,* I thought. *She's an understanding soul.* I sat on the floor and made sure that my toolbox was secured to the floor with extra duct tape, and again surrendered myself to the zero-gravity gods. Suddenly, the plane began its first eye-popping ascent, and I realized that there was no holding back. A vomit bag in my hand, I prepared for another extended round of suffering.

As we pushed over the top of the first arc, I rose off the floor as if being levitated by an all-powerful invisible force. Marveling at how gently the transition to weightlessness occurred, considering that the plane was moving at nearly the speed of sound, I blinked in surprise. *Shit, this is amazing!*

The plane turned over and began its descent, gaining the speed that it had shed as it cruised over the very top of the arc. I slowly settled back to the floor, arriving with a gentle bump just as the jet began its path through the bottom of the parabola. I was pressed into the floor, but to my delight I felt fine. Better than fine, in fact. I was the king of the world; this was suddenly one of the greatest moments of my life! I was starting my second ride on the now Non-Vomit Comet, free to enjoy every aspect of weightlessness and feeling great.

The rest of the trip passed in what seemed like mere minutes. While I did complete the necessary activation and deactivation of all the hardware (and documented that again there were no leaks, failures, or other adverse events), my memories of the flight have very little to do with that technological accomplishment. I tried floating in every conceivable position. I did slow zero-gravity somersaults while successfully remaining within my designated area. I drifted over to the edge of my neighboring team and watched the mannequin suffer through day number two of surgery. I sympathized with individuals in the cabin who were suffering in the same manner that I had the previous morning. I chatted with the NASA technician and convinced her to take my picture in a couple heroic weightless poses.

And most importantly, I walked off the plane once again feeling the need . . . *the need for speed.*

# AND AWAY WE GO

December 20, 1989

**ROLAND, GREG, AND** I walked into what served as a makeshift hotel bar in Kazakhstan and sat at a table. We had spent the past several days at the Baikonur launch facility assembling and loading flight hardware, and early that morning we'd attended the launch of the rocket carrying them to the *Mir* space station. We were tired and ready to relax before a celebratory dinner with our American and Russian colleagues. Having recently given up drinking, I was consuming only mineral water.

The bar was a no-frills affair, as was true of much of what we had encountered in the Soviet Union since our arrival in Moscow one week earlier. A handful of Russians were sitting at the bar with drinks that had been dispensed from a limited collection of bottles behind the counter. Above, a television was tuned to a Soviet state-sponsored news broadcast. As the three of us chatted, we glanced idly at the screen. Then, we became quiet and studied the televised images more carefully.

The commentator was speaking Russian, but the corresponding video feed clearly was originating from a US broadcast. On the television, a map of the Western Hemisphere showed broad arrows extending from the southern United States to Central America. The image then cut to video footage of American troops being delivered to an obviously foreign countryside by helicopters. We next viewed a soundless image of Manuel Noriega accompanied by the deep-pitched delivery of commentary in Russian. We watched the images with open mouths and rapidly increasing nervousness. The Russians at the bar, including a lone hotel employee, were glancing back at us, and then back at the television. We looked at one another, thinking the same question simultaneously. *Did we . . . just invade Panama?*

The fall of the Soviet bloc and communism in Europe had begun and then accelerated in the months, weeks, and finally days leading up to our departure. Events the preceding summer, coinciding with our struggle to successfully test and certify of our flight hardware, had seen the official recognition of the Solidarity political party in Poland and the election of that nation's first non-Communist Party leader since World War II. That profound political event was followed shortly thereafter by the establishment of a new government and free elections in Hungary. Only one month before our departure for Russia, the most iconic moment during the gradual collapse of communism throughout Europe had been broadcast live around the world, as East German borders were opened to the West and the Berlin Wall was pulled down block by concrete block.

As the wall came down, in the nearby German town of Dresden an anonymous mid-level Russian intelligence agent frantically burned incriminating KGB files at the Soviet Culture Center. His name was Vladimir Putin.

Less than one week before we departed Boston, a new government assumed the leadership of Czechoslovakia. The concept of traveling to the Soviet Union at the precise moment in history when each of its satellite states in Eastern Europe were taking turns throwing off Communist rule was somewhat unnerving. My father, who had gradually evolved away from the intransigent conservatism of his younger days, but still expressed enormous disdain for communism and the Soviet Union, had discussed the situation with me, helpfully pointing out that if the situation continued to deteriorate for the Russian leadership, my colleagues and I might find ourselves in Moscow precisely when a Soviet invasion of Eastern Europe and a subsequent war broke out. While such an event seemed unlikely, it was not completely unimaginable. Then as now the Russian military boasted a consistent history of rolling into their neighboring countries with tanks and troops when prior rebellions had tested the country's resolve.

The timing of the mission and our departure also coincided with considerable change in my life and that of my research lab. A few months earlier, Amy had surprised me with the news that she was pregnant. Her due date was in late March of the following year, less than three months after my scheduled trip to the Soviet Union, and squarely coinciding with my timeline for turning in a completed doctoral thesis and then defending it. At roughly the same time, our boss informed his students, staff, and the chemistry department at MIT that he had accepted a faculty position at Brandeis University, about twelve miles west of Boston in the suburb of Waltham. While I would still be allowed to complete my doctorate as a student at MIT, the lab itself would pack up, close, and move in December, precisely as we were boarding our flights to Moscow.

The three of us were not able to entirely avoid the work that was required to move a large academic research laboratory. It became our job to pack up the protein crystallization room and ensure the safe delivery of ongoing experiments to our newly renovated space at Brandeis. We spent two days carefully boxing up and labeling fifteen years' worth of equipment, supplies, and crystallization plates and arranging their transport. Midway through the second day of the process, Roland had the misfortune of fumbling a fluid-filled bottle from a shelf above his head. As it tumbled off the shelf, its lid came off and its contents soaked his head, face, and torso. Reaching quickly for the near-empty bottle, the three of us anxiously scanned it to identify precisely what fluid Roland was now marinating in—a substance which could have easily included any manner of irritants, poisons, or toxins that were commonly employed during our research. The bottle was labeled on its side with a single cryptic inscription: *MR BUFFER*.

The three of us paused and looked at one another, then burst into laughter. "Oh my God!" Roland loudly announced to anyone in hearing distance. "I just drank Mr. Buffer!" The mystery was quickly solved when one of our fellow students, who was working to solve the structure of an enzyme called mandelate racemase, informed us that "MR" was simply his abbreviation for that enzyme. The bottle in question contained his magic solution for its crystallization, which fortunately contained nothing more alarming than a variety of non-toxic salts and water.

After completing that assignment, we packed up our individual desks and benches and left our boxes in the hands of our fellow graduate students for transport to the lab's new home. We then shifted our attention down the street to Payload Systems, where multiple steel shipping containers were being loaded with flight hardware, laboratory tools, supplies, and chemicals. The protein samples themselves would fly in coolers with us, never leaving our sides for the duration of the trip. As we carefully filled and logged the contents of each crate, we noticed that the Payload Systems employees who would be joining us for the mission were loading a final separate container with alcohol, cigarettes, candy, and other sundries. Payload had already paid various Soviet space agencies the necessary agreed-upon fees in full for the experiment, but they were well prepared for any additional, informal bartering that might become necessary once we were behind the Iron Curtain.

The three of us departed together on a late evening flight on Swissair, connecting the next morning in Zurich on a Moscow-bound flight run by the Soviet state airline Aeroflot. The change in comfort level and service between the two flights served as a clear harbinger of what awaited us in the Soviet Union. The sleek new Boeing jetliner that took us to Zurich was replaced by a Russian-built Yakalov that had clearly seen countless takeoffs, landings, and rear ends in its well-worn seats. The outstanding wine and food service on our outbound flight was replaced with green plastic cups of lukewarm mineral water accompanied by stale buns and cheese.

We arrived at Sheremetyevo International Airport in Moscow early in the evening of December 13, exhausted and hungry. Waiting at the airport to greet us were Anthony and two Payload Systems engineers who had traveled a day ahead of us with the shipping containers—a young, female, company-hired translator named Sasha, and several representatives from the Soviet space program. We cleared customs under the watchful eyes of uniformed military officers and plainclothes security and set off into the city.

My immediate impressions of Moscow, as we entered the downtown area, were that its streets and squares were dark and foreboding. The lack of lighting or any obvious sign of festivity that you would expect in a major city in the weeks preceding the holiday season was notable. As we exited our car at the entrance to our hotel, I found the silence and darkness throughout the immediate area unnerving and a bit sinister.

Before departing for Kazakhstan, we stayed overnight at the Hotel Ukraina. The building was enormous. Built over a four-year period in the 1950s, it had been the tallest hotel in the world for twenty years. It was designed in what was called a Stalinist style, with massive stones, steps, and towers housing nearly six hundred rooms and apartments. Images of hammers and sickles, stars, and Soviet workers dominated the walls. While the hotel may have enjoyed a brief period of grandeur upon its opening, at the time of our arrival its original glory had faded. Its plain furniture, threadbare curtains and bed linens, and aged amenities, as well as the presence of a stern elderly hall monitor seated in a chair at the elevator bank on every guest floor, reminded us that we were now guests of the Bolshevik state.

We did not linger in Moscow. The next morning, we were joined by the entire traveling party that would be heading on to the Baikonur launch facility. The Payload Systems staff that would be with us for the remainder of the trip included Anthony, three engineers (Bob Renshaw, the lead project engineer who had guided me through the dark days of hardware testing; Bruce Yost, a young engineer whose rudimentary ability to speak German while drinking a considerable volume of Armenian cognac would soon come in handy; and Julianne Zimmerman, a newly graduated MIT-trained engineer), and our translator, Sasha. Julianne and Sasha were both young, attractive women whose presence would not go unnoticed by Russian officials during our mission.

Our traveling group was rounded out by representatives of Glavkosmos and Licensintorg, who represented the Soviet space program's commercial business interests, and NPO Energia, the agency in charge of the *Mir* space station and its resident cosmonauts. One of the Russians, a silent hulking individual dressed in an ill-fitting suit, appeared to be a bit of an outsider to the rest of his colleagues. We immediately assigned him an imaginary but entirely plausible role within the group as a KGB spy, awarding him the uncreative nickname "Boris."

Our flight to Kazakhstan was also on a commercial Aeroflot jetliner. Aside from our traveling party, the rest of the passenger group appeared to be primarily uniformed Russian servicemen, destined for posting at the military base that was attached to the launch facility. We had been assigned seats scattered throughout the aircraft. I was seated next to a young Russian soldier who appeared to be no more than eighteen. He was clearly intrigued by my presence on the flight, particularly by my bright red, white, and blue parka, which my wife had thoughtfully decorated with a light-up snowman pin. He tried to initiate a conversation, but neither my Russian language skills, which at that point and forevermore would consist of nothing further than a few deliberately learned epithets, as well as *please* and *thank you,* nor his own spoken English ability took us very far towards a diplomatic breakthrough. Visibly satisfied with having met an actual American, my newfound friend finally smiled, leaned back, and went to sleep.

Our arrival in Baikonur occurred without fanfare. Upon landing, the flight crew requested, in both Russian and English, that all passengers remain in their seats while the American delegation and their hosts deplaned. We were led into a reception room in the terminal, where we waited for our luggage and equipment to be off-loaded and placed into trucks. Within thirty minutes, we arrived at the hotel, which would have served nicely as a spartan freshmen dormitory at most American colleges,  and found our rooms. As was the case wherever we stayed during the mission, our passports were collected and stored away, to be returned upon our departure.

Dinner provided an immediate indicator of what awaited us over the course of our stay. I will honestly state that I can count the number of food items that I dislike on one hand. One of those happens to be beets, which as I should have predicted given our destination, would be prominently featured throughout every meal during our visit to the Soviet Union. The myriad ways in which they could be prepared and served were impressive—shredded, sliced, or cubed; roasted, stewed, or boiled; pickled, sauced, or served plain. Nonetheless, my appreciation of the disgusting root did not increase from one meal to the next.

Our first dinner featured, in addition to an unavoidable beet dish, a creamy bowl of what appeared to be a stroganoff. Tasting the evening's entree, I didn't find it objectionable, but it was definitely . . .

unique to my palate. I turned to Sasha and asked her what we were eating. She confessed ignorance and then asked our server during his subsequent pass around the table. A short conversation ensued, during which Sasha's normally cheerful face clouded slightly. She leaned towards me and quietly whispered that I should just think of it as "tasty meat" and leave it at that. After a bit of additional cajoling, I learned that I was consuming my first entrée featuring horse, which, for the record, absolutely does not taste like chicken.

The next morning, we loaded ourselves and our crates into a series of vans and departed the hotel at 8:00 a.m. The narrow two-lane road leading from the town to the Baikonur site was marked by disheveled asphalt, frequent potholes, and stretches of unpaved dirt. Given that this thoroughfare provided the sole automobile access to one of the most important scientific and technical installations in the entire Soviet Union, which was the home of arguably the greatest technological triumphs in its seventy-two-year history, I wondered what the road system was like out in less inhabited and less important hinterlands. Thirty minutes later, we pulled up to a nondescript group of two- and three-story buildings. Gathering outside the entry to one, we were informed that we would be taken to our laboratory space and adjoining conference room. Under no circumstances, we were warned, were we to venture outside of that area without an escort. Even occasional strolls to the lavatory would be monitored by a member of a security group now assigned to keep an eye on us.

We were escorted to our workspace for the duration of the mission. Upon entering, we examined the room. It clearly had not been intended as a lab. It looked more than anything else like a poorly lit day basement in an American suburban split-level home built in the 1950s. Dark faux wood paneling clashed with a mottled grey carpet that had clearly seen a great deal of traffic and activity over the years. The room was outfitted with four plain tables and a mismatched assortment of chairs. A large window along one wall, flanked by curtains that could be closed if desired, provided a view into an adjoining conference room where we would hold any necessary discussions and sign documents prior to turning over the hardware. Our Russian hosts informed us that the space usually served as the dressing room for cosmonauts but had been carefully converted into laboratory space for the American scientific project. *Perfect*, I thought. *Why would we want anything more?*

The rest of the day was spent setting up. We covered tables with aluminum foil and plastic wrap. We taped off and labeled individual spaces for each piece of hardware. Each intended unit and its contents were matched with a backup device, to be identically loaded. The plan was to load one set of hardware with our protein samples twenty-four hours before launch, and then load another the next day to use in the event of a launch delay. If any device showed questionable behavior as it was loaded (for example, if its liquid contents started to drip out the bottom—still a worry in the back of my mind), its backup could be swapped in. Notebooks were set out with printed documentation pages for each device and experiment. By the end of the afternoon, everything was unpacked and laid out in an unassembled state. The plan was straightforward, and everyone was ready for the task at hand. Nonetheless, I was sure that our efforts over the next few days would be accompanied by at least a few moments of unforeseen drama and discomfort. My expectations would not go unfulfilled, but our upcoming challenges, which I anticipated would be caused by Russian inadequacies, would instead prove to be almost entirely self-inflicted.

# BAIKONUR MAN

**A SEPARATE GROUP** had arrived in Moscow to form an official launch observation team on behalf of Payload Systems, as required by the US government. They included Ann Flowers, the lawyer who had led the effort to draft and obtain the necessary export license; Jeff Manber, who had represented Payload Systems at the Commerce Department and had left his governmental position shortly before the mission; and Anthony's own father, Anthony Sr., a physicist and academic research investigator with longstanding contacts in the Soviet Union, who had helped his son make initial contact with Russian bureaucrats over two years earlier. They would gather at the Mission Control Center in Kaliningrad, slightly north of Moscow, to observe the launch and subsequent orbit and docking of the unmanned supply rocket with the *Mir* space station.

While we were subsisting in Kazakhstan with uncooperative flight hardware, beet casseroles, wretched weather, and alcohol-fueled Russian hospitality, our representatives in Moscow found themselves attempting to forge connections with high-ranking officials within the Soviet space program—some of whom were visibly unhappy with the American presence in their midst and the inclusion of our experiments on their space station.

Upon our arrival and laboratory setup in Kazakhstan, the

following two days were spent systematically assembling flight hardware and documenting each device's performance in a final leak test, using a small vacuum bell and pump that we had brought with us. For this first mission, one of the proteins being flown was from my own graduate research work. That protein had been confounding me throughout my PhD training. I had been trying to grow decent crystals of it for three years without much success; the few crystals that I had grown were very small and diffracted X-rays weakly. I had recently taken them to an X-ray synchrotron facility in Great Britain and had examined their behavior on two different beamlines with equally discouraging results. In addition to their poor performance during data collection, a careful analysis indicated that the crystals were poorly ordered internally, with packing defects throughout the interior of the crystals that would prove to be fatal when trying to solve the structure. I had reached a point of complete frustration with the project. In my mind the concept of launching the protein deep into space was perfectly reasonable both scientifically and emotionally.

The first day's efforts proceeded without trouble, resulting in one completed set of primary VD and BLD devices by the end of the afternoon, each flight-certified and deemed ready for sample loading. We had gone back to the hotel that evening feeling satisfied with our progress and game plan. I spent a quiet evening in my room reading until the lack of sleep over the previous several nights caught up with me.

The next day was scheduled to be an exact repeat of its predecessor, in which we would move on to the assembly of backup devices. Those units would not be used if all went according to plan. However, a protocol had been agreed upon with the Soviets that called for us to have backup hardware loaded twenty-four hours after the primary hardware in case of a last-minute launch delay. Under such circumstances, documents would be signed indicating the transfer of backup hardware back to our team, and then the newly filled devices would similarly be transferred to the Russians (a step that would again be documented). It was an uncomplicated plan.

Three hours into the second round of assembly, Greg and I were working with the ever-troublesome BLDs. The first step in the process was the placement of rubber seals into one half of each device before clamping the other half down onto its partner and carefully capturing the seals in their appropriate channels. We had slowly worked our way through the first few of the devices and then paused, noting that there appeared to be a shortage of O-rings that comprised a key part of the sealing system in each device. Greg and I looked at each other, and then casually walked back to the unpacked shipping containers in which we had carefully placed and logged each component of the lab and the flight hardware. The package that was missing was small—no larger than a plastic sandwich baggie, filled with about a couple hundred small black O-rings each less than a centimeter in diameter. Such an item could easily have been overlooked when unpacking, or carelessly set aside in the laboratory.

We found the packing containers to be empty upon our first quick examination, as well as our second more careful search. We strolled the perimeter of the lab, surveying each table for the missing parts. Roland noticed our growing concern and joined our search. We soon were on our hands and knees looking into the corners of the dimly lit room; we then opened and inspected each smaller container, box, envelope, notebook, and satchel. The situation began to register upon the three of us; we had a laboratory full of unassembled flight hardware that was expected to be turned into loaded experimental devices, but we were going to be unable to do so because of a missing envelope containing a handful of small rubber rings. If we had been back in Boston, the situation would have been resolved with a fast trip to the local hardware store. Deep in the Soviet state of Kazakhstan, however, we were screwed.

Bob Renshaw, our lead engineer and my chauffeur during the dark days of device certification, picked that exact moment to enter the lab from the adjoining conference space. While the curtains framing the window separating the two rooms were wide open, nobody in the outer meeting area had yet noticed the quiet drama on the other side of the glass. Bob glanced at our faces and immediately recognized that our previously uneventful lab work had hit a snag. We informed him of the situation. He tilted his head back, stared at the ceiling for a moment, and blew out his cheeks. "Let's go through the room again," he suggested. Fifteen minutes later, the four of us were huddled together, considering our options. We were joined by Anthony, who had also noticed that activity in the lab had paused. A whispered conversation now ensued, complete with hand gestures and facial expressions that any human being could easily recognize as an international expression of a glitch and corresponding frustration.

We came to a decision. "Keep assembling the devices," Bob and Anthony advised, "but obviously don't bother loading the incomplete ones on the final day. We'll hope that the launch goes off exactly as scheduled, and that the lack of backup experiments ends up being something that neither the Soviets nor the rest of the world ever need to know about." If a launch delay were to occur, we would deal with the consequences then.

The engineers and Anthony filed back out of the lab into the conference room and were assessed by their counterparts from the various agencies of the Soviet space program. Our anxious little conversation in the lab had not gone unnoticed, and one of the Russians politely inquired if all was well. "Oh, yes," Anthony replied, assuring them there were just some annoying questions and issues that needed to be agreed upon between the scientists and the engineers. Our counterparts nodded and appeared satisfied with the answer. Clearly red tape, bureaucracy, and disagreements between engineers and scientists were issues they understood perfectly well.

The next day we were greeted by the arrival of a cold front with considerable bite. We would need less time in the lab, as the primary experimental hardware was fully assembled and simply in need of loading. The three of us boarded the vans with our individual coolers of protein samples and again endured the extended bumpy ride to the cosmodrome. As was the case the prior three mornings, the van's windows were obstructed by opaque curtains, which reflected a desire on the part of the Soviets to prevent us from viewing the landscape between the town and the facility. I had stolen a couple glances through a gap between the edge of the window and the curtain and had been rewarded by a panoramic view of empty fields and distant steppes.

We chatted quietly among ourselves about the latest bit of news of the world that had filtered to Anthony during a call with Payload Systems the prior evening. The past two days had seen a series of increasingly violent, bloody riots and military reprisals in Romania. We remarked to one another that yet another domino in the Soviet bloc might fall soon but thought little more of the situation.

The morning was spent loading the primary hardware with solutions of proteins and crystallization buffers, sealing the devices, and conducting final leak tests. Shortly before noon, we turned over the boxes, which were bright, shiny gold rather than black, and relaxed in the rear of the conference room during the handover and final sign-off for the experiments. One of the senior Russian engineers mugged for a camera, pretending to cover his eyes while he signed off on the delivery of the experiments into his colleagues' hands.

Having completed our task for the day, we returned to the hotel for lunch and a free afternoon. Our hosts surprised us by asking if we would like to walk around town. We accepted without hesitation, eager to break from the routine of being under a polite form of house arrest. As part of the tour, we were brought through a local park. There, arranged in a simple square around an abstract sculpture, were plaques with photographs and names of approximately one hundred men—all casualties of the worst disaster in the history of the Soviet space program, the Nedelin catastrophe of October 24, 1960. On that date, a prototype of a Russian ICBM had exploded on the launch pad at Baikonur, killing all the personnel within the range of the resulting fireball. Included in the death toll was the commanding officer of the Soviet Union's Strategic Rocket Forces, Mitrofan Ivanovich Nedelin. The Soviet Union had refused to acknowledge the accident to the outside world until only a few months prior to our arrival in Baikonur. We were probably the first Americans to see the memorial and hear a firsthand account of the disaster.

Our return to the hotel was followed by an informal reception and toasts to mark the milestone of having completed the handoff of our experiments. The next day would require a similarly short effort in the lab, in which we would be ostensibly preparing backup flight hardware while crossing our fingers that those devices would not be called upon. As it turned out, I would have no useful role in, and very little memory of, that final day.

The toasts and speeches (translated in rapid sequence by Sasha) continued through dinner, the evening's beet salad and goulash accompanied by shots of Russian vodka and American whiskey, which Anthony had produced from the special shipping crate. After our meal, we congregated in the lobby of the hotel. Roland, Greg, and I were ready to head off to our rooms, mentally drained from the work of the day and the corresponding laboratory drama. Anthony and Bob drifted over to us and whispered that the Russians had decided that tonight would be when our groups would bond together over further drinks. We demurred, but he was insistent that one of us needed to participate, arguing that to not be sufficiently represented as a team could be taken as an insult of their hospitality. I agreed to stay up and join the group. The rest, as the cliché clearly explains, was history.

*"Baikonur Man!"*

After struggling through breakfast, my colleagues and I boarded a van of uncertain vintage and manufacturer and set out for our makeshift laboratory. With closed eyes and slow, deep breathing, I managed to endure the journey to the cosmodrome over the rough, pothole-filled road. Once in the lab, the curtain was mercifully closed to the outside world. Roland and Greg thoughtfully turned down the lights in the room. We were supposed to be spending our time this morning loading backup devices. The ever-reliable VDs were in fact loaded, while the lucky one-third of the remaining BLDs with intact seals also received their intended protein solutions. The rest were set aside. Upon completion of that task, we commenced the packing up of our portable lab.

I would like to be able to state that I marshalled the ability to participate in our final morning of work. Instead, I spent the entirety of it lying on my back on the floor, the hood of my sweatshirt pulled tight around my head. I was joined in my quiet suffering by Julianne, the youngest of Payload's engineering team, who had also been part of the previous evening's festivities. At some point during the morning, I became aware of Roland documenting our condition with his camera. I responded with a raised middle finger and then returned to a dark quiet place of reflection, repentance, and the first stages of a very slow, incremental recovery.

After finishing up in the lab, we were driven out to the actual launch site to see the Progress resupply vehicle and watch as the primary hardware was taken up the elevator to be loaded into the unmanned capsule. The air was still ice cold, and I noted through my slowly lifting mental haze that thick low clouds and fog were gathering on the horizon. After viewing the rocket and posing for pictures, we were driven to a small obelisk a few hundred yards away, marking the launch site of Sputnik. A small steel replica of the tiny satellite was mounted on the top of the monument over a Soviet seal. Eventually, we returned to our lodging. I excused myself from the group and retreated to my room, leaving clear instructions to not expect me for dinner or any other activity for the remainder of the evening. The launch would occur early the following morning, and I would do everything in my power to be fully present.

# LAUNCH AND RELEASE

**FIRST US EXPERIMENT** SET TO FLY ON SOVIET SPACE STATION

Payload Systems' Protein Crystallization Package to Lift-Off for Mir on December 20

Experiment Aims to Speed New Drug Discovery Process

**CAMBRIDGE, Massachusetts. December 6, 1989 –** The first commercial US experiment to fly on the Soviet space station Mir will be placed into orbit on Wednesday, December 20, it was announced today. The package will be launched on board a Progress re-supply vehicle from the Soviet launch facility in Baikonur, Kazakhstan.

According to Payload Systems officials, the purpose of the experiment is to extend protein crystal growth work to long-duration space flight. The longer duration is essential for many types of crystals to grow. Payload Systems elected to use the Soviet station because it is the only manned facility offering extended time in microgravity. On Mir, the crystals will have three months to grow. The research has applications in facilitating the development of pharmaceutical products and enhancing the effectiveness of currently existing drugs.

Payload Systems is presently the only US company authorized to fly on the Mir Space Station. The company was granted an export license by the US Department of Commerce in February 1988 and has reserved six three-

month experiments over a four-year period.
—Payload Systems Press Release.

I woke up to my alarm early the next morning. Launch was scheduled for 6:30 a.m. I was feeling both better and worse than twenty-four hours earlier. Now more than a day past my introduction to Russian-level drinking, I was sober and had regained a reasonable level of hydration and lucidity. On the downside, the final banishment of alcohol from my system had brought the damage to my body from two nights before into a sharper focus. My bruised right side had blossomed into a stunning spectrum of color, ranging from bright yellow and orange at its fringes to deep purple and black at its center. I also was sporting a significant abrasion on my elbow, another dark bruise on my wrist, and a fingernail that had been torn far into the quick of my index finger. Other than that, all was well.

I ventured into the hotel lobby area and encountered several Payload employees, as well as Greg and Roland. All of them, regardless of how their prior evenings had been spent, looked somewhat drained of their vitality. They smiled encouragingly and asked how I was feeling. "Fine," I responded, and then went on to give them a description of the bodily harm that was hidden under my clothing. Might any of them have an idea of what had transpired during our night of booze and bonding with our Russian hosts?

Bruce Yost spoke up immediately. "Oh yeah," he said. "You had a hell of a fall. You'd just made a second or third toast for our everlasting friendship. You were walking out of the sauna and towards the pool when your feet went straight up in the air and over your head, and you slammed down on the deck like a crash-test dummy."

"For a moment, we really thought you'd hurt yourself," he continued, "but you bounced back up and yelled 'I'm all right!' to everyone in the room." The Russians, he noted, had seemed quite impressed.

Having solved the mystery of my injuries, I turned my attention to the morning's coming launch. It was scheduled in about ninety minutes, at 6:30 a.m. I mentioned my growing anticipation of the event, and the group became a bit quieter. Renshaw and Anthony looked down, and then Bob spoke. The fog outside was so thick you couldn't see more than about ten yards. The likelihood of an on-time launch seemed remote—as did the opportunity to walk away with our heads held high and our incompletely loaded backup hardware quietly packed away, never to be mentioned to our Russian friends.

The ride to the observation station near the launch pad was understandably slow, as the driver of the van was reduced to nearly a walking pace due to the impenetrable fog, which seemed to be growing thicker by the minute. Departing from the vehicle, we assembled on a platform, unsure of which direction the rocket was located. We were joined by multiple military and space agency officials. The discussion quickly turned to the weather, and our doubts about a launch were translated to our hosts. They looked at us with a clear sense of amusement. "Nonsense," they conveyed through our translator. "A little fog is nothing to worry about. We've proceeded in far worse than this." Slightly reassured, we waited.

The moment of launch was unaccompanied by any warning or visual cue. Nonetheless, the sound of the liftoff conveyed overwhelming power and energy. The roar and vibration of the rocket as it rose from the pad shook my organs, teeth, and eyeballs, and it felt as if the launch pad was within a stone's throw of our location. I would later learn that we were standing over a mile and a half away. A single photograph that I had taken at the moment of launch would show nothing but a uniform dark grey cloud. Greg, Roland, and I looked at each other and smiled. We had just listened to a Soviet rocket liftoff, carrying our American experiments, and in so doing had accomplished a milestone in the history of human space exploration and science, as well as US–Soviet cooperation.

We had all reacted as if it were business as usual.

Over a thousand miles away, at the Soviet mission control center outside of Moscow, our observation team had assembled to view the launch remotely. As recounted by Jeff Manber in his book, they also noted that the weather at Baikonur was dismal and expressed the same skepticism for a successful launch from their balcony seats at mission control. After the launch, they watched the flight trajectory on a large telemetry screen until it had reached orbit. The mission director then turned to the Americans. "There," he said. "You can see it is done. Now, let us eat breakfast."

Back in Baikonur, we returned to the hotel for breakfast and started to think about our return to Moscow and then the US. The progress capsule was due to dock with *Mir* in two days, on December 22. The plan was to return to Moscow and join the observation team at Mission Control for the transfer of our experiments to the space station, then to all fly home in smaller groups on December 24. I was ticketed to fly to Frankfurt on Aeroflot, then to Chicago on Lufthansa, and then finally into Moline, Illinois on a short commuter flight, where I would be joining Amy and her family in time for Christmas Eve.

Our excitement at the successful completion of our part of the mission was dampened by the news that we would be unable to leave Baikonur for at least a day, as the weather was simply too poor for flights to land at the local airport. While the Soviet space program might have no problem launching rockets under conditions of zero visibility, apparently Aeroflot did not have the same confidence or capability. We spent the day in a somewhat restless fashion, with little to do other than socialize. I had finished the reading material that I had brought with me for the trip and cursed myself for not packing extra books. Some limited drinking was going on; having decided that I would never again drink for the rest of my life, that activity held no interest for me. That afternoon, we were invited to go on another walk around the town. This time, we strolled around the main residential area, which consisted of large unadorned apartment buildings that primarily housed military families and those of the staff working at the cosmodrome and its launch facility. The overwhelming color of both the town and the sky was grey, the weather uncomfortably cold and damp. We ended our walk with a quick look inside a Soviet grocery market and found it to be just as spartan as one might have imagined.

That night, the Soviets put on a substantial dinner banquet to celebrate the first stage of our success. The commanding general of the military base joined us, wearing his dress uniform and an impressive array of medals and commendations. Within minutes of his arrival, he had singled out Julianne and Sasha, rarely leaving their sides for the remainder of the evening. The meal was, by the standards of our prior dinners, a great spread, featuring fresh fruit, smoked fish, black Russian bread, and of course new and imaginative forms of beet preparations. At the banquet table, I had carefully positioned myself between Greg and Julianne, to avoid a Russian dining partner who might wish to trade toasts with me. More Armenian cognac was opened. I struggled to not let its nauseating odor detract from the evening's sense of accomplishment.

The next morning, we all assembled again, ready to depart for the airport and a flight back to Moscow. Again, we were informed that we would remain in Kazakhstan for at least another day while waiting for the fog to lift. We looked at one another with a bit of dismay. *This has been terrific*, I thought, *but I'd really like to get the heck out of here now.*

The day was again spent under communal house arrest. Our hosts, having run out of sites in the town to examine, nonetheless gamely invited us for another walk at midday. Having nothing better to do, we accepted and dutifully trudged through the town square again. After returning to the hotel, we were asked if we would like to watch a movie. "Sure," we said, "why not?" Gathering in the banquet room, a large television of Russian vintage  was connected to a VCR. Within a couple minutes, the erotic American movie *Nine and a Half Weeks* was playing overdubbed in Russian, with all the characters' lines spoken by a single male narrator in a deep, serious voice. As Kim Basinger succumbed to the attention of Micky Rourke, her vocal responses to his physical attentions were translated and articulated in a Russian baritone. The effect was both disturbing and hilarious.

Dinner that night was a much more subdued affair; it was clear that our hosts were just as ready for our departure as we were. That night we adjourned to our bedrooms in a state of heightened anxiety: the weather report was unimproved, as were the chances of a flight out.

The next day, no offers of walks, celebratory meals, or overdubbed sexy American movies were provided. We sat around the hotel listlessly, realizing that the docking of the Progress capsule with *Mir* and transfer of our experiments would likely occur early that evening while we were still stuck at Baikonur. As dinnertime approached, one of our hosts approached Anthony and Sasha and spoke to them quietly. They listened closely, then turned to the group. "Grab your suitcases," Anthony said simply. "We're leaving right now."

The Russians had indeed grown weary of trying to keep us fed and entertained and were also running low on supplies. The hotel had been stocked for a week's stay, and we were  now three days past our scheduled departure. As I passed Sasha in the hallway to grab my possessions and jacket, I asked her what the plan was. The Soviet military, she replied, is bringing in a troop transport plane to extract us from Kazakhstan. Apparently, the Russian Air Force could fly where Aeroflot would not.

In less than an hour, we were loading the company's shipping crates and all our personal luggage onto a large military jet sporting the hammer and sickle. We were shown to the front of the plane and into an officers' cabin directly behind the cockpit, which was separated from the enlisted troops' seating farther back. We placed our crates and bags in the cabin, and then turned them into footrests as we took our places in bench-style seating that ran both sides of the area. Seats at a single table were occupied by Anthony and one of the Glavkosmos representatives. Within minutes of boarding, the plane was in the air.

Upon landing in Moscow, we went directly to a celebration in our hotel, already in progress, of the capsule's docking with the space station. We walked into the room to a loud cheer followed by a call for new rounds of toasts. The observation party had returned to mission control earlier that afternoon to watch the transfer of our experiments and new supplies into *Mir*. Tomorrow, we would all go out again together, to be present as the experiments were activated. At the end of the evening, some of the group headed out into the Moscow night to continue celebrating the success of our mission and many future partnerships between American companies and the Soviet space program. I remained behind.

Before going to bed that evening, I searched out the hotel bar and TV to try to catch up quickly on world events. As before, I was able to glean a bit of information from the Soviet broadcast, but without the same level of comprehension that had accompanied the images of the US invasion of Panama days earlier. However, a small group of English-speaking businessmen gathered in the same area provided an alarming update of new events in the rapidly crumbling Soviet bloc, now entirely focused on the Republic of Romania. After ordering the open rebellion against his regime to be violently quashed only six days earlier, the Romanian dictator Nicolae Ceausescu had briefly left the country, returning a day later to escalating riots and protests. While military troops unsuccessfully attempted to establish order, the country's situation descended rapidly into open warfare in the streets. By the time of our arrival in Moscow, Ceausescu and his wife had tried to flee and been captured. They now faced trial and a very questionable future.

I was shocked. While other Communist Party governments in

the Soviet bloc had fallen over the past months, none had resulted in the level of bloodshed being described in Romania, much less the arrest and possible execution of their leaders. It was not hard to imagine the level of paranoia that was probably descending on the Russian leadership, not far from our hotel at the Kremlin. The next day, I would see for myself.

# ESCAPE FROM MOSCOW

### *December 23, 1989*

**I AWOKE WITH** a start. Heavy shades were blocking much of the morning's light from penetrating the room. Nonetheless, I could see a shadowy figure pacing at the foot of my bed. Having gone to sleep alone soon after the end of the celebratory gathering at the hotel, I was unsure who was in the room with me. I had expected to be joined by a roommate for the last couple evenings in the Soviet Union but wasn't sure who it might be. Hearing me stir, my mysterious room partner turned towards my bed. It was Jeff Manber, formerly of the US Commerce Department and now a member of Payload's observation team in Moscow. I had met him for the first time the night before.

Jeff was still in the grip of the previous night's libations, a condition that I could easily identify with. He sat heavily on the end of my bed, stared at me with wide eyes, and related some of the details of his prior evening. He had gone out into the cold December night with several companions, including Anthony. They had eventually found themselves at a bar about a mile away from the hotel where they had been befriended, as Jeff repeated emphatically several times with wide eyes, by "gangsters and pimps and prostitutes." Eventually he had left the party and had managed to navigate himself back to the hotel and then up to my room, which apparently was now our room. He had no idea where Anthony was, or even if he was still alive. I yawned, stretched, and stated that if anyone could successfully navigate a sketchy evening in the Soviet capital it was our leader.

Within an hour, we had joined our group (including a very much still alive and surprisingly alert Anthony) in the hotel lobby for breakfast and then rode together to Mission Control. For the observation group, it would be their third trip there in four days. For those of us who had just arrived from Baikonur, it was our first visit. We rolled past block after block of grimy industrial facilities and apartment buildings, all presenting uniform grey concrete exteriors to passersby.

Upon our arrival at Mission Control, a heavy metal gate was opened by an elderly attendant, providing entrance to a courtyard area in front of a nondescript three-story building. As we stepped off our bus, I squinted at our surroundings. I had previously visited US Mission Control in Houston, and during my time there had enjoyed the museum, visitors' center, rockets on display (including a full sized, flight-certified Saturn V), and of course touring the space center itself. Here, Mission Control was just a rusty gate, a grizzled attendant, and a large, unmarked solitary building.

Entering the structure, my initial impression of the command center for the Soviet space program shifted dramatically. Whereas from the outside their Mission Control center was unremarkable, inside it was much more spectacular. Marble walls, high ceilings, ornate chandeliers, and a massive statue of Lenin greeted us. The entrance to the actual control room was lined with pictures of all the men and women who had flown with the Soviets, including several Americans who had been part of the historic docking of Apollo and Soyuz capsules many years earlier.

We were shown to a receiving room that had been set up for family members of cosmonauts to occasionally visit and speak to their loved ones. The room was appointed with paneled walls, comfortable padded chairs, and a microphone system and speakers for conversations between Earth and *Mir*. Our translator, Sasha, was given the microphone, and soon was casually chatting with the cosmonauts in Russian, their responses booming from the speakers. Then, Sasha handed the microphone to Jeff and encouraged him to say something.

Aware that he was suffering the aftermath of his first serious Russian drinking experience, I perked up and listened carefully. After a moment's concentration, he offered a perfunctory wish for good relations and successful business between our countries. *A man of international commerce to the end,* I thought. He followed up his statement with additional wishes for the cosmonauts' safe return to the planet Earth.

His comments, completed before 10:00 a.m., were accompanied by the opening of a fresh bottle of Armenian cognac. I concluded that Glavkosmos must have gotten an excellent wholesale deal on that specific form of alcohol.

After our morning visit to Mission Control, we returned to our hotel and were told that the remainder of the day and evening were ours to occupy as we wished. Having recently endured a week-long, carefully regimented and closely guarded visit to Kazakhstan, I was excited. I've always enjoyed walking by myself in new cities, so I strolled out of the hotel and into Moscow's streets with a vague plan. I was scheduled to board my flight out of Moscow early the next morning and intended to spend my remaining hours in the Soviet Union exploring the grounds surrounding the Kremlin and its corresponding museums and sites.

I quickly realized that I would not be able to easily blend with the local population. It was a Saturday, only two days before Christmas. While the city was not obviously decorated in recognition of the holiday season, large numbers of pedestrians were out and about.

The weather was mild, but I was bundled up in a manner appropriate for a stereotypical bitter Russian winter. Beyond my American blue jeans, which by themselves provided ample reason for attention, I was wearing the same large, puffy, red-white-and-blue winter jacket that had previously attracted attention in Kazakhstan. While most people on the sidewalks were dressed in dark grey or brown winter jackets, I was a walking advertisement for the United States of America. To further ensure that I would not go unnoticed, the jacket was still adorned with the large snowman pin with light-up eyes that Amy had thoughtfully attached to a pocket.

It was only a matter of minutes before I was being asked by strangers to sell my jeans to them. Other individuals that didn't offer to relieve me of my pants in exchange for rubles nonetheless went to great lengths to make eye contact and offer smiles, head nods, and salutations. While it was unnerving to suddenly be the object of a crowd's attention, nobody persisted in following me to an alarming degree, and I had no trouble walking along the crowded sidewalks.

Eventually I had made my way to the edge of Red Square. It had not been easy to do so, as the density of the crowd had increased significantly in the last block or two leading to the open space. Directly in front of me, over the heads of last few layers of gathered people, I could see the walls and towers of the Kremlin. Slowly working my way forward, I noted that the crowd had become quiet and that nobody was moving forward. As I reached the front of the throng of people, I saw that barricades had been erected at the street's end, clearly to prevent the populace from entering Red Square.

The public space itself was empty, except for the presence of several military trucks and corresponding troops distributed around the perimeter. Two armed soldiers were standing on the opposite side of the barricade directly in front of me, calmly surveying the crowd. I placed my hands on the barricade and looked at Red Square in confusion. For a moment, I tried to understand why the center of the Soviet capital would have been closed. Was a holiday event about to occur? Was the crowd that I was now part of waiting for some sort of performance? A Christmas pageant, perhaps? Across the way, I could see similar crowds gathered at different streets and walkways that would normally empty into the plaza, all blocked by similar barricades and groups of soldiers.

One of the closest guards had fixed his gaze on me. He took in my obviously foreign (and likely American) clothing, cocked his head slightly to one side, then smiled slightly. I suddenly felt compelled to ask a question. "I want to visit the Kremlin museums," I found myself telling him. "Do I need to buy a ticket?" As soon as the words were out of my mouth, I realized how utterly foolish they were. Clearly, no tourists were going into the Kremlin today for fun. The guard gazed as me impassively. Then, he spoke three words in mixed Russian and English: "Nyet Red Square."

I stood at my position for a while longer, staring at the scene around me. *Of all the shitty luck,* I thought. *I come all the way to the Soviet Union, spend all this time here, finally have one open afternoon, and I can't go see Lenin or the Fabergé eggs.*

After another minute or two of observation, the nature of the situation gradually dawned on me. Just a few days earlier, a gathering in front of the Communist Party headquarters in the Romanian capital had rapidly grown into a nationwide protest and insurrection that had swiftly led to the downfall of the government and the subsequent pursuit and arrest of that country's dictator and wife. In less than another twenty-four hours they would be tried, convicted, and summarily executed by a firing squad in the middle of a public sidewalk. The leaders of the remaining Soviet empire— likely gathered inside the building looming in front of me—were scared. My irritation over having my tourist plans interrupted were suddenly replaced by the realization that I was witnessing history in the making. The beginning of the end for Russian communism was taking place as I stood at the edge of Red Square and watched.

I eventually turned around to try to work my way back through the crowd and head back to the hotel. As I did, I noticed a young boy standing next to me, holding the edge of his mother's coat. He was staring up at me with wide eyes, taking in my brightly colored jacket. His mother was likewise assessing me and my garb. I looked more closely at her child and saw that he was staring at the snowman pin. I reached up and turned on the switch that activated his lights. Then, I took it off and handed it to him.

The next morning was Christmas Eve. By about 7:00 a.m., I had joined a group from Payload Systems that was scheduled to depart on various flights leaving in close sequence from Sheremetyevo International Airport. Anthony, Bob, Bruce, Julianne, and Sasha were flying back to Boston; Ann Flowers and Jeff Manber were flying to London and then on to the States. I was scheduled to travel alone, first to Frankfurt and then on to Chicago. The final flight, a short commuter hop, would put me into the Moline, Illinois, airport in time to meet up with Amy and her family for late Christmas Eve. Later in the day, Roland and Greg were scheduled to fly together back to the US.

The eight of us were picked up by a van and joined by a Glavkosmos representative named Anatoly. The drive to the airport was quiet as it was still at least an hour before sunrise, and the streets were as dark as ever. Arriving at the airport, we immediately noticed that the expansive ticket counter area and surrounding cavernous lobby was in chaos. The weather throughout much of eastern and central Europe had been wretched for several days, and flight schedules were in disarray. Crowds of passengers who had experienced cancellations packed the hall and surrounded every available agent and desk. I noted that there was no semblance of orderly queues, and (not for the first time) I felt an appreciation for my own countrymen. *Americans may have many faults,* I thought, *but they understand the purpose of a single-file line.*

Fortunately, I already had my paper tickets in hand, along with my passport, and would not need to try to deal with the problems facing the crowds of people now trying to make new travel plans. I turned towards the departure area without checking the status of my own departing flight.

There were two stages of security that we were required to pass through to make our way to the gates. Anatoly offered his best wishes and goodbyes to us all. One at a time, we presented our passports and exit visas to a guard at the first checkpoint and answered a few questions about the duration and purpose of our stay, again under the watchful eyes of both uniformed and plainclothes security agents. Once our exit visas were taken from us, we were now on a one-way street back home; there was no turning back to the USSR. We proceeded on to the second checkpoint, another thirty feet towards the gates, where we would have our tickets examined and be issued an actual boarding pass. I stood last in line, watching my comrades check through. I then stepped up myself and handed over my passport and ticket. The attendant examined it, then looked at his screen. My friends on the other side stood gathered, waiting for me while chatting amongst themselves.

He looked up at me. "Sorry sir," he said in clear English. "Your flight to Frankfurt is cancelled."

I stared at him, not quite comprehending what he had just told me. "Are you sure?" I asked. "Absolutely," he replied. "You'll need to go back and obtain a new ticket. Truly, you should have checked the flight status before you cleared passport control." I pondered this information. Several issues rapidly coalesced in my mind. First, I had already turned over my exit visa, so I was unsure that I could casually stroll back into the ticket lobby. Second, even if I could, how would I venture to begin fighting my way through the mobs of Soviets that were packed ten- to fifteen-deep around each ticket desk, and make myself understood to the airline agent?

My friends looked at me sympathetically from their vantage point on the other side of the checkpoint. As a group, they smiled in encouragement, waved tentatively, and disappeared towards the gate area.

I turned around and started to walk back towards the ticket counters. As I approached the first checkpoint, the security guards gazed at me impassively. One held up his hand. "Nyet," he informed me. I sighed and stopped, considering my options. I was a traveler in no-man's land—can't leave and can't easily go back. I considered simply lying down on the floor in the neutral zone to see what the eventual response might be. Looking both ways, I saw that the guards at each station were now watching me.

I closed my eyes tightly for a moment, struggling for a moment of clarity. Few constructive or positive thoughts surfaced. Opening them again, I suddenly spotted Anatoly standing at a security railing, casually observing me. Rather than immediately depart, he had lingered, probably under orders to ensure that we proceeded to our gates and truly left the country. He looked at me with a pained expression then beckoned me to return to the ticket lobby. I started to walk toward him, still rolling my suitcase. He quickly shook his head and pointed at my bag. *Leave it there*, he was clearly indicating. Without hesitation, I left it fully unattended and sitting by itself in the open space between checkpoints and strolled purposefully back past passport control, without stopping to ask permission or explain myself. I was surprised to not hear raised voices ordering me to halt.

Anatoly grabbed me by the sleeve and guided me toward one of the ticket counters. We were at the back of a large crowd that was gathered around a single overwhelmed agent. I noted that while the group was in physical disarray, with no obvious order or priority, they were relatively quiet and stoic. I realized that such situations were probably not uncommon in the Soviet Union, and that these people had learned throughout their lives that verbal tantrums would do little to solve their immediate problems.

Anatoly, a tall man, was in a better position to assess the situation. Suddenly, he yelled a short burst of Russian in a deep, authoritative voice over the crowd and at the lone airline employee. My ears made out several words. *Amerikanski! Glavkosmos! Mir!* The crowd quieted even further and turned around collectively to look at us both. Then, the gate agent yelled back at him. Anatoly turned to me. "Give me your passport and a credit card," he said. I dutifully pulled out both and handed them over. He placed the card inside the passport and handed it to the stranger in front of him. My eyes widened as I watched my sole forms of finance, identification, and international travel authorization disappear into the crowd as they were exchanged from one hand to another.

A few minutes passed, then a credit card charge slip traveled back to us, again being transported in a hand-over-hand, bucket brigade fashion. It was followed by a ballpoint pen. I glanced at the slip and saw that I was being charged for a one-way ticket to London's Heathrow Airport. I quickly signed, and then handed both slip and pen back to the person in front of me, who passed them forward; they continued on, disappearing into the crowd ahead. A few minutes later, I could see my passport and credit card each working their way back in my direction. Following immediately behind them was a freshly printed ticket on a flight out of Moscow, bound for London.

I looked at Anatoly with a combination of amazement and gratitude that I have very rarely felt towards any human being before or since. He held out his hand and took mine, gave it a solid single shake, and pointed back toward the passport checkpoint. Thanking him, I turned and started back. I could feel the eyes of many in the area still watching me. I walked up to the same guard that I had now passed by twice, wondering what would happen next. He also seemed unsure; I felt it was unlikely that he had experienced very many travelers so blatantly breaking the rules of departure from the

Soviet Union. He looked at my passport a second time, then glanced at a superior, who was standing behind him. The officer looked at me briefly, then gave a gentle nod. I was free to proceed.

I collected my suitcase from where it had waited for me unmolested during my brief return to Mother Russia and proceeded onwards to the second checkpoint. Within minutes I had a boarding pass for the London-bound flight, due to leave in less than an hour. I walked away and down the corridor towards my gate, gripped with an overwhelming sense of relief.

Waiting at my gate were Ann Flower and Jeff Manber, who were also flying to London. They were delighted and clearly surprised to see me. Ann's pleasure at seeing me increased when I noticed that she was clearly hungover and offered her one of three bottles of Russian Pepsi that I had put in my suitcase to take home as souvenirs. Jeff took a photograph that would one day hang prominently in my office. It shows Ann and me sitting side-by-side—her holding my Pepsi, me holding my boarding pass. Both of us look triumphant.

Two weeks later, I was reunited with Roland and Greg. They informed me that when they arrived at the airport later that day and made their own way through passport control and exit security, the paperwork they carried that indicated their own association with Payload Systems and Glavkosmos had induced considerable amusement on the faces of airport security. Only after hearing the story of my escape from Moscow did they realize that it was my blazing such a unique and memorable path through Sheremetyevo Airport earlier in the day that had turned their own departure into a source of extra attention and entertainment.

The remainder of my trip through London, then on to Chicago on another newly purchased ticket on British Airlines, then finally on my original scheduled flight to Moline took the better part of twenty hours. When I finally arrived, my very pregnant wife and her family, who lived fifteen minutes from the airport, were late.

# CRYSTALS IN SPACE

**PAYLOAD SYSTEMS INC.** Prepares for Return of Mir-Grown Crystals

**Experiment is First American Payload on Soviet Space Station**

Lon Rains

Space News

February 1, 1990

Payload Systems, Inc. is preparing for the return in February of the first American payload ever to fly on the Soviet space station Mir, a mission likely to pave the way for at least five additional flights.

The protein crystal growth experiments were launched December 20 from the Soviets' Baikonur Cosmodrome. The 58-day experiment will be deactivated February 19 by cosmonauts Alexander Viktorenko and Alexander Serebrov, who will bring the payload back to Earth on a Soyuz TM spacecraft when their tour on board Mir ends February 24.

The next mission on Mir could come later this year, said Vinit Nijhawan, chief operations officer of Payload Systems. However, no date will be set until the first payload has been successfully returned to Earth. So far, the company has been more than satisfied with the Soviet ground crew and the performance of the cosmonauts, said Nijhawan. He said the company's contract with the Soviets originally called for activation of the experiments within seven days of the launch.

But, when the cosmonauts learned that the Payload Systems crew which had been in the Soviet Union desperately wanted to go home for Christmas, they altered their schedule and activated the experiments on December 23.

Also, he noted the mission was launched in a dense fog. "I think that says something about their reliability."

Once the cosmonauts land, they will take the payload with them on a helicopter and deliver it to the Payload Systems crew in the Soviet Union. The crystals will then be photographed again before they are flown to the government's Brookhaven National Laboratory on Long Island, N.Y., where they will be analyzed.

After a week in the Midwest recovering from my wounds and celebrating the holidays, Amy and I had returned to Boston where we dove into a whirlwind of activity that would continue for the first six months of 1990. I was finishing writing my PhD thesis and was planning to turn it in and defend it in late March. Meanwhile, Amy (now entering her final two months of pregnancy) continued to work as an administrative assistant at the Massachusetts General Hospital. Our crystallization experiments would be returned to us in late February. Together with Roland and Greg, I would take the devices to an X-ray synchrotron facility at Brookhaven National Laboratory on Long Island and collect diffraction data as part of an assessment of the effect of microgravity on their growth and performance.

Looming over those plans was an impending move to the West Coast at the start of the summer. I had secured a postdoctoral research position at the University of California in Berkeley and would be starting in the middle of August. Roland was similarly completing and preparing to defend his own doctoral thesis and would also be moving to the West Coast, taking up a similar postdoctoral position at the California Institute of Technology in Pasadena. Finally, Greg was finishing his own short postdoctoral stint in Wisconsin and preparing to assume a faculty position at Penn State University. Like others in our field of research, his success in solving a new structure of a protein while in graduate school had greatly accelerated his timeline to an academic appointment as a tenure-track assistant professor.

I was writing my PhD thesis in a laboratory room at Payload Systems, rather than driving out to Brandeis University each day. My first day back, I was greeted by Anthony, Bob, and Julianne, who had last seen me stranded in the middle of the departure area of Sheremetyevo Airport. My story of how I escaped that situation reduced them to tears of laughter. Walking into the lab, I was confronted with the still-unopened equipment crates that had returned from Moscow. I opened them each and systematically restocked the remaining supplies and equipment on the neighboring shelves. There, they were joined by the missing package of O-rings, which I had found waiting innocently on a table where they had accidentally been left behind.

Our plans for my remaining time at MIT were interrupted in early February by Amy's realization one afternoon that she was not feeling our baby move. Immediately, we made an urgent appointment at the prenatal clinic at Beth Israel hospital, where an exam indicated that the baby was still healthy but mom was experiencing preeclampsia. By the end of the day, Amy was home and on enforced bedrest, restricted to lying on her left-hand side for the remainder of her pregnancy. For the remaining few weeks before the birth of our son, she would be allowed out of bed only to eat, bathe, and use the restroom. I selfishly took advantage of the situation by bringing her fresh drafts of my revised doctoral thesis chapters each evening to examine for misspellings and grammatical errors. By the time the document was turned in, its construction and use of English neared to perfection.

The return capsule carrying two cosmonauts and our crystallization hardware landed in the steppes of Siberia on February 24, and were returned to Payload Systems engineers in Moscow a day later. Once the crystallization hardware had been returned to us, Roland and I spent days carefully opening, photographing, and characterizing the crystals in each device. We were relieved to see that crystals had in fact grown, having been reminded of the shuttle mission a few years earlier in which almost every experiment had failed. We had no idea exactly what the environment on *Mir* would be like and worried that some combination of heat, humidity, and vibration would conspire to kill the crystals before they could grow.

However, they really didn't look much different than what we were growing with the same protein solutions on Earth. Physically, they were the same basic shape and size. If there were to be any improvement, it would be in how strongly and sharply they diffracted X-rays. We mounted the best of the space-grown crystals and the corresponding Earth-grown crystals into quartz capillaries, and on a cold Monday morning in mid-March we left Boston for Brookhaven National Laboratory on Long Island, where we were joined by Greg. Normally, we would have driven to the Connecticut coast, taken a ramshackle ferry across the Long Island Sound, and then driven the remaining distance to the facility. This time, however, our travels were being paid by Payload Systems, so we flew in style from Boston to the regional airport in Islip, New York.

We spent several days collecting X-ray diffraction images from crystals grown in space and on Earth and processing the resulting data, which would need to be examined and compared. After about three days, we were getting close to the end of the specimens that we had brought down and were starting to think about returning home.

Then a phone call from my sister-in-law, who had come out

to watch over Amy during my absence, relayed the news that her pregnancy was approaching the moment of truth. Within minutes I had informed Greg and Roland that they would be finishing up the data collection without me and was out the door and on my way to the local airport, where I caught the first available flight bound for Boston. A day later, Amy delivered our first son, whom we had decided to name Benjamin. Three weeks afterwards I presented and defended my doctoral thesis to a group of four faculty members in a small classroom on the MIT campus. The outcome was far more positive than what occurred the same day in Kenmore Square, where the Red Sox absorbed an 18-0 loss to the Milwaukee Brewers.

Shortly after my thesis defense, the Baikonur team met again at Payload Systems to review the results of our analyses and to outline plans for the next mission. We compared photographs of the crystals taken on *Mir* when the experiments were deactivated, then again in the USSR after the return of our devices, and then finally in the US upon their delivery to Cambridge. They had withstood their travel from orbit back to Earth without any obvious problems. We went on to discuss parameters and protocols needing improvement before the next flight, including better quality of photographs of the crystals in the devices, and further work to optimize the materials and fabrication of crystallization devices. We also made the easy decision to discontinue our use of the troublesome BLD devices and to instead concentrate entirely on crystallization experiments using only the vapor diffusion method and corresponding, more reliable VD devices.

No sooner had we committed those most excellent plans to writing than a bombshell memorandum arrived from Anthony:

> As a result of the management meetings and the Board of Directors' meeting held in recent weeks, we have reluctantly concluded that we cannot go forward with the Mir Protein Crystal Growth venture as an internally funded project.

While the Mir space station does possess scientific merit and commercial potential, the financial requirements of running the program properly are too great for the company at this time.

We plan to continue investigating a number of outside financing options in the hope that the venture can be continued. However, in the meantime, we must prudently wrap up the program. Our objectives are to minimize company expenditures while preserving the integrity of the program so that it can be restarted when appropriate. This requires an immediate curtailment of all non-essential program activities, thorough recording and archiving of all program data, and cost-conscious monitoring of those activities which will remain ongoing.

Attached to the memorandum was a list of steps to place the program into hibernation, while potential governmental or industrial partners were courted who might provide the necessary financial backing for a second mission. Beyond a complete accounting of all the hardware, data, and records from the first mission, and plans for a manuscript documenting our results, the last activity I would participate in before leaving Cambridge was a final project meeting in early June. Anthony initiated that final gathering by reiterating that any funds that would enable us to fly mission two would not come from Payload Systems or its parent company, and that marketing efforts over the summer would determine the future of the program. He went on to state that pharmaceutical companies whom he had hoped would eventually represent deep-pocketed future customers were out of the question, whereas a few space-oriented organizations were showing some interest. He had made contacts with several possible suitors, including governmental space agencies from Canada, the Netherlands, and France. Also included in the list, for unclear reasons, was the Japanese computer company Fujitsu.

The remainder of the summer, while Amy, Ben, and I were slowly driving across the country to our new home in the Bay Area, my colleagues dutifully continued to pursue potential partnerships. Greg worked on a co-authored research article detailing the results of the first mission's crystal growth experiments, which we had drafted over the past month.

Because of the sheer amount of X-ray data to be processed from the crystals we had grown on *Mir*, that manuscript would not be submitted for publication at the *Journal of Protein Crystal Growth* until a year later, in the fall of 1991. It was eventually published on December 15, exactly two years to the day after we first arrived at the Baikonur Cosmodrome for the first mission. Entitled "Long duration growth of protein crystals in microgravity aboard the *Mir* space station," the article concluded with a statement that microgravity might not cure all problems associated with protein crystal growth, and that it should be thought of as simply another variable to be considered when designing crystallization experiments.

Well before that study was published, while my family and I were in the middle of our cross-country trip, our activities and plans were succinctly summarized in an article in *Business Week*, for the entire world to consider.

A Hitchhiker on Russian Rockets
Can US-based Payload get off the ground with Moscow's help?
Gary McWilliams
Business Week
July 2, 1990

A few years ago, a small Massachusetts company called Payload Systems Inc. saw an opportunity in packaging scientific experiments for flights in space. It hoped to use the space shuttle, but that fell through with the 1986 Challenger disaster. The outfit took the next best step: it went to the Soviet Union. The Soviets had a space station called Mir, plus a desperate need for hard currency. For under $1 million, they accepted a 56-day experiment that Payload funded itself.

Scientists studying everything from microchips to lasers see advantages in space labs. That should provide a good niche for Payload. They are among several companies designing space experiments and lining up the earliest possible flights. Payload will charge up to $1.5 million a mission, but it claims the benefits are worth it, and underwrote the experiment on Mir to prove the point.

It was only 20 months from the original contract . . . until an unmanned Soviet rocket Progress ferried Payload's experiments from the Baikonur Cosmodrome in the eastern republic of Kazakhstan. Such quick response will mean nothing, however, unless Payload can lure clients. That's why it chose drug research for its first ride—in hopes of attracting pharmaceutical companies. Scientists in those firms are struggling to shorten the process, which sometimes takes decades, of developing new drugs, a process that relies on understanding the complex structure of the protein target. The best bet is X-ray crystallography. Attempts to grow the best possible crystals have led scientists to try growing crystals in the weightlessness of space.

Eventually, similar experiments might be performed on the US space station Freedom, which is to be assembled and conducting research by 1995. But for now, the Soviets have cornered the market on long-term crystal research in space.

The article concluded with a dramatic flourish:

For those willing to pay the freight, Payload has lined up the best lab in the galaxy.

While I was amused by how the author had apparently determined the state of laboratory science throughout our entire galaxy, it was certainly true that we had access to the only platform that was continuously in orbit around the Earth. As I drove my family westward that summer, I considered what we had accomplished in such a short time and on a shoestring budget. The partnership between Payload Systems and the Soviet space program might have been held together with faith and duct tape, but I felt that with another mission and more experimental tests, we might settle our own questions about the value of zero gravity for protein crystallization. I hoped that Payload Systems and its leadership would find a way to keep the band together for at least another year or two.

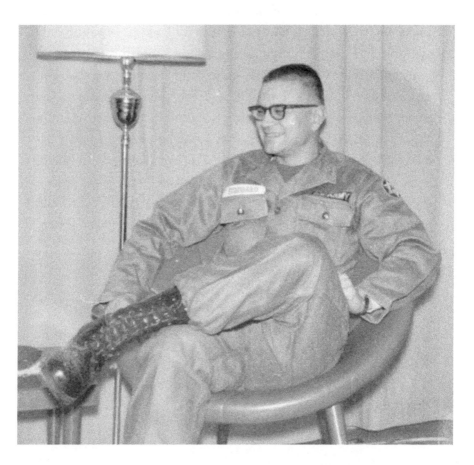

I was born shortly after my father's discharge from
the US Army 35th Engineers combat battalion, for
which he was trained both as an amphibious invasion
beachmaster and as a 'nuclear demolition' specialist. He
came very close to actually having to apply the former
training on the Cuban coast in October of 1962.

# Department of the Army

## Certificate of Training

### This is to certify that

2D LT CHARLES L STODDARD, 05705333

AS A MEMBER OF THE 35TH ENGINEER XM-41 ASSEMBLY TEAM

### has successfully completed

AN ATOMIC DEMOLITION MUNITION TECHNICAL PROFICIENCY INSPECTION,

CONDUCTED BY THE CONARC INSPECTOR GENERAL'S TEAM ON 27 NOVEMBER 1961.

### Given at HEADQUARTERS, 35TH ENGINEER BATTALION (COMBAT)
FORT LEWIS, WASHINGTON

8 DECEMBER 1961

JAMES A CURRY
LT COL, CE
COMMANDING

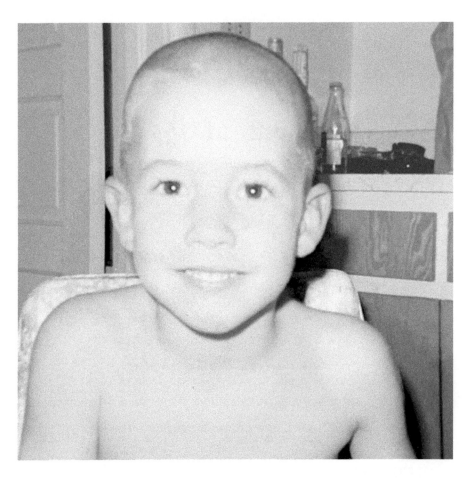

Growing up in the woods, mountains and waters of Northern Idaho in the 1960s and 70s was a great time, even if a military-grade haircut was still a firm requirement.

The 'Great Dome', located at the front and center of the MIT campus, serves as Tech's most visible and iconic image.

The lab and several of its collaborators, including myself and Greg Farber (front left and right) at an X-ray synchrotron facility in Hamburg Germany, shortly before our first mission to the Soviet Union.

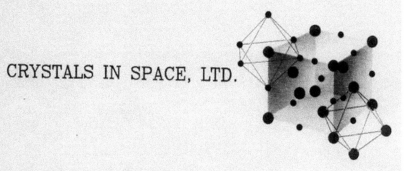

# CRYSTALS IN SPACE, LTD.

A subsidiary of Petsko North, Inc.

Roland K Strong, President

Gregory K. Farber, CEO

Barry L. Stoddard, Chairman

****Better Crystals for a strong America***

This hastily constructed placard hung on the door to the lab annex where Roland, Greg and I worked together from our first meeting with Payload Systems until the lab's departure from Cambridge at the end of 1989.

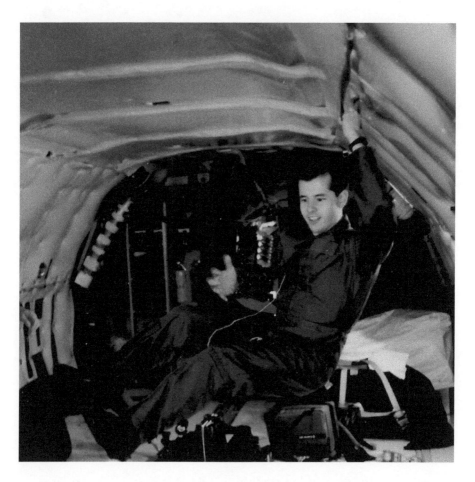

NASA's KC-135 Bounce Flight, also known as the 'Vomit Comet', represented a demanding test of resilience for both the flight hardware and for its operator.

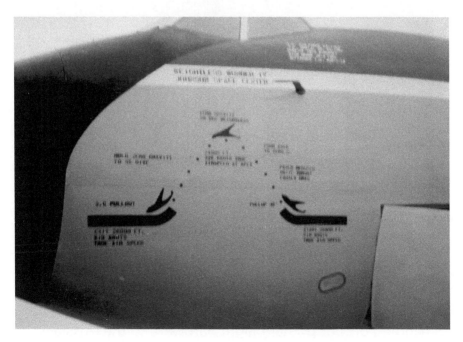

133

Our improvised lab set up at the Bakanur Cosmodrome. Greg and Barry work on the assembly of the ever-troublesome BLD devices.

We all pose with a checklist for three devices upon handing off our primary flight hardware to the Russians.

After our first couple days, Bob Renshaw (in the middle) and two Russian engineers inspect assembled crystallization devices.

The day before launch. We gathered at the supply rocket as the payload was loaded into the capsule. My All-American parka and jeans stand out in the group.

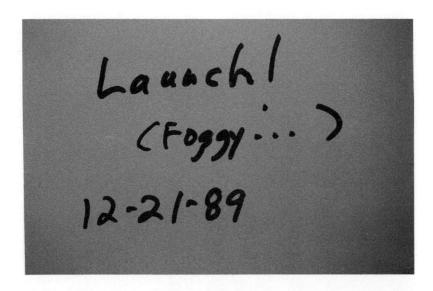

By the next morning, a photograph pointing directly at the sound of the launch produced nothing but a view of impenetrable fog.

After several extra days unexpectedly confined to our lodging we were finally flown out of Kazakhstan in the officers' cabin of a Russian military transport. Left to right: Anthony, Bruce, Sasha and Julianne.

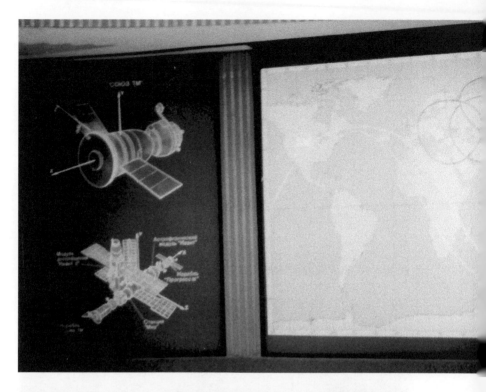

The day before our departure from Moscow, we visited
Soviet Mission Control to witness and celebrate the
activation of our experiments.

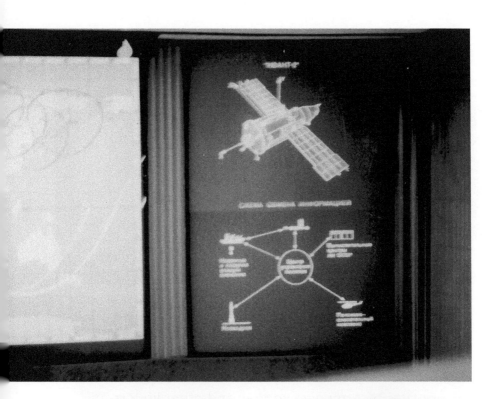

**ВИКТОРЕНКО**
АЛЕКСАНДР СТЕПАНОВИЧ
КОМАНДИР
"ВИТЯЗЬ-1"

**СЕРЕБРОВ**
АЛЕКСАНДР АЛЕКСАНДРОВИЧ
БОРТИНЖЕНЕР
"ВИТЯЗЬ-2"

The photograph on the wall was of the two cosmonauts
(Aleksandr Viktoenko and Aleksandr Serebrove) who
activated and then returned the experiments to earth.

The Baikonur team poses alongside Russian colleagues for one more round of toasts. Those who were still recovering from prior bonding opportunities managed to smile bravely in the face of yet more freshly opened bottles of Armenian cognac and other liquors.

December 23, 1989. An empty and barricaded Red Square, closed off to crowds on all sides to avoid potential anti-communism demonstrations, on the eve of our departure from Moscow.

Christmas Eve. My last-minute procurement of a boarding pass to London (complete with a very creative spelling of my last name) finally allowed my exit from Moscow.

On the flight with me was Ann Flowers, who was rejuvenated by a timely gift of a Russian Pepsi from my suitcase.

January 1992: Roland and Chris pose in -20° weather
in Moscow, partway on our walk to Red Square and the
Kremlin museums. While both of my colleagues were
well insulated against the Russian winter, I was woefully
underprepared.

Launch of the supply rocket carrying our experimental hardware for Mission Number 2 on a clear and bitterly cold morning in Kazakhstan. The rocket was out of sight in a matter of seconds; I snapped three pictures before its disappearance.

# PART 2:
## AFTER THE FALL (1990 – 1993)

"Whether you like it or not, history is on our side. We
will bury you."
—Nikita Khrushchev

"The biggest thing that has happened in my life, in our
lives, is this: by the grace of God, America won the Cold
War."
—George H.W. Bush

"If you try to fail and succeed, which have you done?"
—George Carlin

# BERKELEY

August 2, 1991

**IT WAS APPROACHING** 10:00 pm on a Friday night, and I was getting ready to go to bed when we suddenly heard running footsteps on the street outside, accompanied by a low rumble that grew steadily louder. As we paused and listened, the windows of our house began to shake.

Amy and I had moved into a rental property a few blocks south of the University of California in Berkeley in early May. Less than a month after we had taken up residence in the two-story, three-bedroom Craftsman-style bungalow, our second son was born. The days since then had been a blur of nighttime feedings, diapers, naps, and postdoctoral research, which I had been pursuing for the past year. We had put both boys, who were slightly more than a year apart in age, down to sleep a couple hours previously, and then stayed up a while longer while I caught up on some notebook entries describing the results of the week's work. Included in the research projects demanding my attention was preparation for mission number two with Payload Systems, which was now less than six months away.

The rumbling and shaking intensified. We opened the front door and surveyed the scene. Dozens of young people, some appearing barely old enough to be in middle school, were running down the sidewalks and street, pausing momentarily to look backwards, sometimes with the objective of throwing a rock or bottle at their pursuers. Following them were several lines of police officers on motorcycles, slowly riding three abreast down the street, herding the crowd towards the Berkeley waterfront and the San Francisco Bay. Their engines at low throttle produced the rumble that rattled the houses to either side. The battle for a nearby parcel of land, known locally as People's Park, which had been fought off and on between the university and many of its neighbors for over twenty years, was currently back on. At stake this time was a volleyball court.

We had arrived in the Bay Area one year earlier, after a cross-country drive lasting several weeks that had been extended by numerous visits with friends and family along the route. I had driven most of the way myself, with Amy usually in the backseat next to our infant son. Our first month on the road culminated in a mid-July family wedding in Minnesota, after which we accelerated our pace, driving to my parents' house in Seattle over the course of four more days. After staying with them briefly, we turned south on Interstate 5 and drove the remaining eight hundred miles to Berkeley, including a final stop in Portland to visit my grandparents.

We initially settled into a two-bedroom apartment in El Cerrito, a working-class suburban community located about two miles north of the University of California. We had traded our third-story walk-up apartment in Boston's Symphony Hall neighborhood for a smaller two-bedroom unit in an aging courtyard-style apartment complex in the East Bay. We had also exchanged the short distances, high population density, and heavily used MBTA transit system that we had taken for granted in Boston for Californian sprawl and the much more modern but far less heavily used BART train lines connecting the Bay Area. I felt lucky to have found an apartment that allowed me to get to campus without having to drive, instead commuting on my bike into Berkeley and back home each day.

I had learned almost immediately upon starting my postdoctoral position that events in Berkeley could be just as extreme as its historical reputation implied. One morning during my very first week in town as I rode toward the campus, I noticed a black helicopter hovering. It was slightly before 8:00 a.m. on a Friday morning, and I was pedaling briskly through the residential neighborhoods that flanked the train line running from the northern East Bay area down to Berkeley and beyond. Drawing near to the college campus, I could hear multiple sirens in the vicinity. As I turned onto Hearst Street and started my final uphill push towards Barker Hall and the research lab, several police cruisers raced by.

Within a couple hours of my arrival, my new lab mates were present and setting up their day's experiments. This morning, however, productivity slowed as news of the events of the past several hours trickled in. Slightly after midnight, a local hotel bar one block off campus had been taken over by a lone individual armed with three guns and hundreds of rounds of ammunition. After immediately shooting several patrons (one of whom, a senior at the university, would later die), the gunman had taken dozens of the customers hostage.

The shooter, who would later be determined to have been in the grip of a severe schizophrenic episode, had demanded trillions of dollars from the US government as payment for services he had previously rendered as a telepath. In lieu of cash, he had gone on to suggest that he could instead be provided ownership of three US states of his choosing. He also demanded that the chief of the San Francisco police department appear on live TV and pull his pants down. Hundreds of police from the region eventually converged on the hotel. Early the next morning, near the time that I was arriving onto campus, the incident ended when law enforcement stormed the hotel bar, shooting the gunman twenty-four times.

After that dramatic start to our time in California, we had settled into a rhythm. The one thing that we did not miss at all about

Boston was its weather, which was best described as six months of frigid winter cold followed immediately by six months of sweltering heat and humidity. If there were two intervening seasons involved, they had been short-lived and hard to notice, let alone enjoy. The Bay Area and Berkeley, in contrast, were heavenly: cool and foggy in the morning, then usually sunny and pleasant in the afternoon, with little difference throughout the seasons apart from occasional rainy spells. No air conditioning was required to stay comfortable. Amy and Ben were out and about every day, mostly on foot to the surrounding stores and a multitude of parks and playgrounds.

My new lab quickly proved to be everything I had hoped for, with several outstanding postdoctoral fellows matched by an equal number of university graduate students. I was now working for Dan Koshland, a legend in the fields of enzymology and protein chemistry. He was an opposite of Greg in many ways; a senior statesman of academic research with over forty years of professorial experience, generally soft-spoken and measured, and keenly in touch with the day-to-day experiments going on at each bench in his lab. He was also a dedicated family man married to a fellow UC Berkeley professor, with whom he had raised five children while eventually becoming one of the most influential scientists in the country. In contrast, Greg was young, brash, single, and as a matter of personal policy, usually wished to hear about his trainees' efforts and results only when they had done something useful and noteworthy.

In one important way, however, Dan and Greg were similar— they both constantly generated new ideas for projects and experiments and freely shared their frequent brainstorms with everyone in their laboratories. For those who could churn through them and then identify and run with the good ones (which often were great), both labs were excellent training grounds. The two men were also well acquainted with one another. Over the past ten years they had occasionally sent their recently graduated PhD students to the other's lab for postdoctoral training—most recently yours truly. Their immense respect for one another was clear; there is little  more precious to an academic research professor than his or her own graduate students.

I had come to the Koshland lab with a specific plan to broaden my research training, hoping to learn several approaches that I had missed out on at MIT. While in Greg's lab, I had focused entirely on protein crystal growth and X-ray crystallography. The closest thing to experimental biochemistry that I had done was to dispense protein solutions, usually already purified and sent to us in the mail by collaborators, into crystallization trays. In Berkeley, I was intent on learning the basics of gene cloning, protein expression and purification, and the study of enzyme function. I had suggested to Dan that I would like to work on two separate projects, like how I had operated in graduate school.

The first project, which I had described in a fellowship proposal for a private foundation that eventually funded my postdoctoral salary, was to study the mechanism by which a protein found on the surface of a cell transmitted a signal from the outside environment to its interior (causing the cell to respond by moving towards the source of the signal). The second project was to use an enzyme being studied in the Koshland lab as a model system to conduct "time-resolved" crystallography. By using ultra-fast flashes of extremely intense X-rays, we could try to visualize a biochemical reaction occurring in real time.

What I had not yet told him is that I would also be working on a third project  that would almost immediately and then regularly take me back to Cambridge, and eventually around the world to Japan, Moscow, and finally back to Kazakhstan.

When we met one last time at Payload Systems before the start of the summer, my continued role in the continuation of Payload's microgravity protein crystallization project was unclear. Roland, Greg, and I were all moving far away from Boston and from each other, and the future of the project depended on industrial and/or governmental partners being found who would pay cold hard cash in exchange for flying their own protein crystallization problems in our hardware. While such partnerships would probably take time to assemble, Anthony was hopeful they could do so. In the meantime, he wanted to keep our team together. Would we be willing to remain involved in return for a consulting fee? He warned us that the compensation they would be able to offer was minimal.

I had no problem doing the necessary mental math. I had just received an offer that would pay an underwhelming sum of $19,700 per year to work as a postdoctoral research fellow. Coupled with that, Amy had decided to stay at home with our new baby rather than returning immediately to work. Therefore, my postdoctoral salary would be all that stood between us and homelessness while I pursued research and continued to train for the next few years. I had already determined that reasonable housing could be obtained somewhere near the Berkeley campus for not much more than $600 per month. Would Payload Systems be willing to pay me an amount that would cover a reasonable portion of our rent? With no hesitation, a handshake deal was struck. For the next two years, I would be paid $6,000 per year by Payload Systems as a consultant.

My first trips back to Boston to continue the process of planning for mission number two were in September and then December of 1990, the first occurring only a few weeks after my arrival in California. Those trips would be followed shortly after the new year with a trip to Japan, where I would meet with scientists at a computer company interested in partnering with Payload Systems for the next flight opportunity.

Shortly before my first trip back East, I asked to speak to Dan in his office to tell him of my plan to take a few days off. At the same time,

I planned to outline the likely scenario of several additional trips out of the lab over the next year or two, which would probably culminate in an extended absence while I traveled back to the Soviet Union. Knowing that time spent in the lab and corresponding scientific productivity are the two forms of currency that are most important to a laboratory supervisor, I was nervous about his response.

I had another reason to be anxious about our conversation; I also needed to inform him that Amy would be having our second baby the following summer. Only a few weeks after our arrival in Berkeley, Amy had called me in the lab late one morning. The phone had been answered by a fellow postdoc, who yelled across the lab that my wife needed to speak to me. I was in the middle of setting up an experiment and removed my gloves with an irritated sigh. Picking up the phone, I brusquely asked her what she needed. With no preamble or warning, she informed me that we would be welcoming a second child in about seven and a half months.

I was later informed by my bench mate, after I returned to my ice bucket and tubes with a dazed expression, that he had not believed that the concept of the blood draining from a person's face could be an actual, visible phenomena. At that moment, however, I was shocked to the core. Our first son was only six months old, still nursing and usually waking us up more than once a night. Neither Amy nor I could remember a moment over the past several weeks when either of us had possessed either the energy or a transient moment of mutual libido that would have resulted in a pregnancy. How had this happened? I decided that there was no way that I would be able to conduct a decent experiment for the rest of the day. Putting away my samples in a lab freezer for the next day, I left the lab and took a very long walk.

Later that week, I knocked on Dan's office door and was greeted by a friendly invitation to enter. He loved to talk to his postdoctoral fellows and was almost always happy to be interrupted by them. His stories and anecdotes of his life in science were limitless and highly entertaining. He had gone to graduate school at the University of Chicago, where his studies were temporarily interrupted by the need for young chemists to participate on the Manhattan Project, carrying out experiments that would lead to the isolation of purified fissionable material for the first atomic bombs. His tales of working with radioactive isotopes and world-renowned chemists during that time were the stuff of legend.

That morning, however, he was visibly distracted. His wife, Marion, a fellow professor at the university, had made an unannounced visit to his office earlier that morning in search of contraband. She worried enormously about his health and forbade him from partaking in unhealthy foods. Dan, who possessed a considerable sweet tooth as well as a substantial appetite for cheeseburgers and fries, had responded by hoarding candy bars in his office and frequently sneaking off to a nearby fast-food joint. As I entered, I could see that Marion had systematically gone through his drawers and shelves looking for his stash. The similarity to a prisoner who had just had his cell flipped by a jailhouse guard was uncanny.

Dan put a couple final notebooks back on the shelves and then settled into his chair. He smiled broadly, unworried about his most recent encounter with marital law enforcement. He asked about my recent round of experiments, which had involved collecting X-ray data on crystals of our favorite enzyme at an X-ray synchrotron facility located near Stanford University, about fifty miles south and across the bay from Berkeley. For that purpose, I had convinced the university administration to allow me to drive a departmental, state-owned pickup truck to Palo Alto and back over the weekend, arguing that my work constituted official business on behalf of the State of California's university system. Dan was appreciative of my broad interpretation of UC-Berkeley policy.

I gave him a quick update on what I had done at the facility and described what the next steps would be for the project. Then I turned to the matter at hand, asking him if he had followed the news of the

American scientific projects being flown on the Russian space station, and if so, if he was fully aware of my ongoing involvement with them.

Dan was in fact well aware of the project and its status. I should not have been surprised. Aside from his immediate scientific interests he was a bit of a Renaissance man and a polymath, conversant in many different areas of science and society. Beyond that, he was also the editor-in-chief of the weekly journal *Science*, which was published by the American Association for the Advancement of Science and served as a preeminent publication of significant new scientific accomplishments and research activities around the world. There was very little in the arena of scientific research and discourse that he was not aware of.

I quickly explained to him that Payload Systems was working towards a second mission and had asked me to continue to work with them as a consultant. There would be more trips over the coming months, I went on, some of which might take me out of the lab for rather long stretches of time. I would do everything possible to maximize my productivity in the lab in the weeks between those trips, but I felt it was important to see the project through.

I had no reason to be nervous about Dan's response. He was a scientist's scientist in every way and expressed nothing except keen interest and a little bit of jealousy at what I described to him. He asked only that I be willing to share my stories with him and the lab when the time was right. Reassured, I followed up that part of the conversation by adding that Amy and I were expecting an addition to our family. Dan received that news with the same graceful aplomb, supplemented by an honest expression of congratulatory excitement. He and Marion had parented five children over the course of their early research careers, the last two of whom (twins) had also been unplanned and unexpected. "That's why her nickname is 'Bunny,'" he told me with a wink. I left Dan's office feeling reassured that all was well and congratulating myself for having again found just the right person to work for during my years of scientific training.

# PLANES, TRAINS, PROTESTS, AND WAR

## January 14, 1991

**I WAS STANDING** in the courtyard outside of Barker Hall, chatting with several fellow postdocs and students. We were being prevented from entering the building due to a chemical spill on the top floor, and it was unclear if we would be able to get back in for the remainder of the day. It was my last day on campus for a while, as I would be boarding a flight for Tokyo the next morning, and I was hoping to wrap up a final experiment and spend time with an undergraduate intern who had been assigned to work with me.

The campus that morning had been crowded with students, staff, and Berkeley locals, mostly within the confines of Sproul Plaza. That area, serving as the most prominent entrance to the campus, had a long history as a site of regular demonstrations and reprisals dating to the early 1960s. In 1964, months of protests and speeches on the plaza aiming to overturn the university's prohibition of political advocacy and fundraising (other than the Democratic and Republican school clubs) had resulted in mass arrest of hundreds of students. Eventually, a new administration had designated the area, and the steps leading to the administration building on its east side, as an open discussion zone for all causes and groups.

The subsequent use of Sproul Plaza for demonstrations during the Vietnam War and surrounding social upheaval peaked with the events of "Bloody Thursday" on May 15, 1969, when a rally and march to protest the conversion of a local People's Park into an athletic field quickly grew into a violent day-long battle between police, students, and local residents, culminating in one fatality, dozens of hospitalizations, and hundreds of injuries. Five days later, a renewed demonstration in the plaza was suppressed with tear gas dispensed from National Guard Helicopters circling above. The *Washington Post* would later editorialize that "indiscriminate gassing of a thousand people not at the time in violation of any law seems more than a little excessive."

Now, twenty-two years later, impending US involvement in a new war was front and center in the minds of many of the university's students and staff, along with their more immediate objections to significant upcoming tuition increases and never-ending tension surrounding the university's continuing desire to develop People's Park. The preceding August, shortly before our arrival in Berkeley, the Iraqi Army had invaded neighboring Kuwait, leading to immediate condemnation and sanctions by a broad collection of Western and Middle Eastern nations. Within weeks, American and British forces, joined by those from Saudi Arabia and Egypt, had been deployed to the Middle East in the largest military coalition since World War II. Joined by live news broadcasting teams embedded with fighting units and reporting in real time, it seemed clear that a massive battle would eventually result—the first significant warfighting by US troops in a generation.

Tensions were running high on the UC Berkeley campus in early January. Students had just returned from the holiday break to be greeted by a series of grim stories and forecasts published in the university's newspaper, *The Daily Cal*:

> Berkeley students fear military draft: Sophomores report phone calls from selective service
> Arabian desert shaping up as war zone: US troops ready themselves

Grim fate lies ahead for US soldiers in the gulf, military experts predict

I had paused in Sproul Plaza briefly on my way across campus, dismounting my bike to walk through the throngs of people milling about. A platform had been set up for speeches later in the day, and campus security was taking up positions around the courtyard. As I slowly walked through the plaza, a singular voice carried across the area from the direction of Ludwig's Fountain. Named after a professor's dog who years before had adopted the fountain as his personal kingdom and playground, the fountain was now a favored site for impromptu outbursts and exhortations by a local Berkeley icon known as the "Hate Man." This morning, he stood on the edge of the fountain, watching and occasionally berating a group of students who were paying various amounts of attention to his presence.

Even by Berkeley standards, the Hate Man was a truly original character. Born Mark Hawthorne in 1936, he had been raised in Connecticut and had served in the US Air Force after graduating from the state university. After completing a tour of duty as an intelligence officer, he had worked for a decade as a reporter for the *New York Times* until 1970, when he had suddenly quit his profession, his marriage, and his family and embarked on a lifetime of deliberate downward mobility and self-chosen homelessness. He moved to Berkeley and created his own personal philosophy of "oppositionality," centered on the idea of being completely open and honest about negative feelings. Dressed in a floppy hat adorned with flowers, an ankle-length woman's skirt, and an ancient khaki jacket, he often greeted newly met individuals with an unsolicited "I hate you!" I would eventually learn that this statement, which he offered frequently and was the origin of his moniker, was quite deliberate.

He argued that the opposing statement of "I love you" was too often used as a form of emotional manipulation, and that "I hate you" was vastly preferable to "We hate them."

Over the years he had generated a substantial following of acolytes. Frequently he and his troupe would be found in a nighttime drum circle known as the "hate camp." I initially  encountered him on the edge of campus during my first week in Berkeley, where he was  amusing himself heckling a bullhorn street evangelist, who were among his favorite targets. I couldn't stop laughing as each evangelical exhortation was met with an even louder rejoinder. "You must be born again!" was followed swiftly by, "Once was too many in your case!" I quietly studied him again this morning, as he surveyed the growing crowds in the plaza, his piercing eyes sweeping across the groups of students. I felt that this morning, more than anything, he looked tired and bored.

The next morning, I boarded a nonstop flight out of San Francisco airport, bound for Tokyo. It was my first trip to Asia, and I was excited. Payload Systems was sending me as their lone representative to meet with researchers and staff at Fujitsu Incorporated, whom they hoped to convince to join mission number two as a corporate partner. There, I would hear about their own work in protein structural studies and try to convince them that microgravity protein crystallization was an area and technology worth their time and money. In addition to my personal bag, I was also carrying a traveling case with prototypes of our crystallization hardware for an inspection, which I would leave with scientists at the company for two weeks. I would then repeat the entire trip, retrieving our devices for transport back to Payload Systems and further assessing their interest in working with us.

On the surface, Fujitsu seemed an odd choice to participate in our studies. Founded in 1935, they were the second oldest information technology company in the world, formed shortly after IBM under the original name Fujitsu Telecommunications Equipment Manufacturing. Over their subsequent fifty-six-year history, they had worked their way to the top of the information technology sector, manufacturing Japan's first computer and then partnering with (and often acquiring) computer manufacturers and IT companies around the world.

As part of their focus on information technology, the company had diversified their R&D portfolio into a variety of disciplines; one was the use of protein crystal structures for the purpose of computational drug design and related pharmaceutical research activities. They had an active protein crystallization research group located on their campus outside of central Tokyo that was working on some of the most challenging problems in the field. My focus would be to describe our own studies and approach to crystallization, learn about their research, and convince them to sign up. Assuming they agreed to join us, I would eventually serve as the traveling scientist who would take possession of their protein samples, transport them to the Baikonur launch facility, and load them into our next round of crystallization experiments.

My request to be seated in the non-smoking section of the wide-body 747 had been granted, but barely. The main floor of the passenger cabin was divided into a forward smokers' section and an aft non-smoker section that were divided by a thin cotton curtain. I was seated in the first row of the latter area, with only a few feet and a single wispy sheet of see-through fabric separating me from several dozen dedicated cigarette fans. Before we had reached cruising altitude, a blue haze of tobacco smoke, nicotine, and tar was settling around me for the duration. Flashing back to long childhood road trips in the backseat of our family sedan, with both of my parents chain-smoking in the front seat, I resigned myself to my hazy and foul-smelling fate and buried myself in a newly purchased book.

I arrived in the late afternoon at Narita International Airport after the twelve-hour flight and caught a shuttle bus to my hotel in downtown Tokyo. My first impression of the city was of ubiquitous bright neon signage and masses of people on the sidewalks that rivaled the Vegas strip. The next morning, I found the local subway station and followed directions that had been provided to me for the train to catch, and the stop to get off, that would bring me to the Fujitsu research campus.

Early the next morning, after finding the appropriate platform at the massive underground station, I watched with wide eyes as throngs of passengers disembarked from arriving trains and then were replaced with groups of equal size. Unlike subways in the US, where the number of people packed into each car was a matter of collective group decision-making, I noted that the Tokyo method of maximizing train capacity was more directly enforced. As the cars filled with humanity, uniformed station attendants with white gloves joined together to push the final passengers into each compartment.

I boarded with a large case of flight hardware in hand. As with the prior train, our car was loaded to a point of bursting. I was amazed at the stoicism of my fellow passengers and their ability to avoid eye contact and maintain personal decorum as they were forced into intimate contact with complete strangers on all sides. I let go of my hardware case, which I had been holding to my chest with both hands, and let my arms drop to my sides to reduce the space that I was occupying. The container never touched the floor, being held next to me for the duration of the thirty-minute trip strictly through the pressure of other bodies pushing against it and myself.

At Fujitsu, I was met by a security guard who escorted me to a conference room next to a laboratory, where a group of five investigators introduced themselves. They seemed surprised at my youthful appearance. Although I would soon be turning twenty-eight and had a wife and child (and another on the way), I still looked as if I were in high school. We spent the next hour chatting pleasantly about our work, our travel experiences, Japan, and the US, with no mention of Payload Systems or crystallization in outer space. I would eventually come to learn and appreciate the Japanese cultural norm of establishing a connection and rapport with a potential new colleague and partner before engaging in business, but at the time I found it disconcerting. Surely Payload System would not be pleased if I returned to California having made some nice new friends, but without any indication of their interest in our project.

Our chat eventually did shift into our experience and results from the first crystallization experiments on *Mir*. I walked them through the numbers, which had come into sharper focus since leaving Boston. The most important result was that all the experiments that we had flown had yielded crystals, in both types of devices, and that the crystals had been shown to diffract at least as well, if not somewhat better, than those grown on Earth. We planned to move onto more challenging systems, including those that were not yielding useful crystals in our own laboratories, for the second mission. I produced our crystallization hardware as I was going through our data and passed the devices around. Eventually, they gathered around one end of the table, engaged in a rapid-fire conversation while trying out the activation knobs on each and holding the devices up to the light. I had no idea if their conversation was trending in the direction of interest or disdain.

The most senior member of the research team looked at me and smiled. Would it be possible, he asked, to adapt the use of our devices for a different crystallization strategy, for a very different type of protein system? Without hesitation, and without asking for any additional details whatsoever, I nodded affirmatively. *Shoot first*, I thought to myself, *and ask questions later*. My counterpart went on to describe their project and question in more detail. They were working to crystallize a large, membrane-bound protein complex, he explained, in which the proteins were dissolved in a mixture of water, salts, and detergent. Furthermore, their preferred crystallization strategy was to simply mix all the proteins and the reagents together at the beginning of the experiment and then let nature (and crystal growth) take over. The method was referred to as "batch" crystallization. More traditional methods of equilibration had been ineffective.

I considered their system and proposed method; their approach could certainly be accommodated in our setup. I informed them that the materials in the devices were compatible with the components of their protein solutions, and then went on to explain that after mixing the protein and crystallization solution in our devices in the Baikonur lab, they would not reach microgravity for about forty-eight hours, but after that they would have two months on the space station for crystallization to occur. Because their crystals were very slow growing, the Fujitsu scientists seemed to accept that the experiment could still work.

By the end of the meeting, it seemed possible that a deal could be struck that would satisfy the needs of the company researchers, and that I could report back to Payload Systems that they should feel free to negotiate a contract with confidence that the scientists would deliver as promised. I was taken out for lunch by company officials, and then placed on a train for another closely packed, cheek-to-jowl trip back to downtown Tokyo. The hardware and its case remained at the company; without its presence next to me I was packed even closer to my nearest neighbors on the train than I had been on my earlier outbound trip.

I was up early the next morning in preparation for my afternoon departure and overnight flight back to California. After a leisurely breakfast in the hotel restaurant, I had packed up my suitcase, and then gone for a long morning walk in the capital city. It was cold with grey skies, heavy cloud cover, and a light mist pressing close to the rooftops of the city's buildings. I spent the better part of two hours walking, including a circumnavigation of much of the grounds of the Imperial Palace. I returned to the hotel by late morning with the intent of a final shower and then a shuttle ride to the airport for my afternoon departure. I turned on the TV, which was tuned to the BBC international news station.

As the screen came to life, I was greeted by images of missile and anti-aircraft fire, explosions, and mayhem in the Iraqi capital of Baghdad. The coalition attack on the Hussein regime had begun while I was on my walk. I sat on my bed and watched in silence as the commentators described the initial salvos in the war, which were intended to reduce Iraq's ability to coordinate a defensive response, as well as induce what was described (and forever embedded into American jargon) as "shock and awe." Sitting on the other side of the world, I certainly felt a bit of those emotions myself.

A couple hours later, while riding to the airport, our bus was diverted to a nearby parking strip about a mile from the terminal; armed security guards boarded the vehicle and asked for us all to produce our passports and tickets. While the Japanese did not have a highly visible presence in the military coalition now acting to drive the Iraqi forces from Kuwait, they were a part of the recognized Western powers aligned with the US and were taking few chances on acts of violence or terrorism on their soil.

I returned to Berkeley and the surrounding Bay Area and found the area's anti-war activists to be energized by the start of the conflict in the Middle East. One senior graduate student and friend of mine, working for a collaborator's lab on the upper campus, had participated in a protest march onto the upper deck of the Bay Bridge, shutting down traffic during the morning rush hour. In return for his troubles, he was arrested and spent several days incarcerated  in San Francisco before being released on his own recognizance. Returning to his lab on the Berkeley campus, where he had been on the threshold of solving the structure of his own protein, he found that his supervisor had rewarded his political activism by taking away his PhD project and giving it to two of his closest friends. They went into overdrive to ensure that they would solve the structure during my friend's absence, eventually assuming the first two authorship positions on the resulting research article, and ultimately enjoying the rewards that accompanied it without shame or apology.

# A RIOT OVER HERE AND A COUP
# OVER THERE

## August 2, 1991

**AS I WALKED** across Telegraph Avenue towards our local supermarket, I glanced to my left towards the university campus and Sproul Plaza, located six blocks to the north. Halfway between, a block off the avenue, was People's Park. As I crossed the street, I noticed that it appeared much busier than usual, with pedestrians milling on the sidewalks and crossing the thoroughfare at a run. Then I noticed a fire burning in the middle of the avenue closer to campus. Puzzled, I wondered if a late summer evening street celebration was underway. By the end of the evening, I realized that I had much to learn about our new home and the extremes of social and political discourse in America.

We had moved from our apartment in El Cerrito into a small three-bedroom house in downtown Berkeley in May, only a few weeks before our second son was born. We had immediately taken to the new location. Living on a quiet residential street just a block and a half off Telegraph Avenue, I could get to and from campus in less than three minutes by bicycle, and Amy could take our son Ben on daily adventures throughout the community. Within weeks, many of the locals, including members of our neighborhood's entrenched homeless population, were inquiring about our toddler's wellbeing during their daily walks.

Amy had sent me out on a Friday evening quest for a pint of ice cream. After taking in the action down the avenue, I jogged across Telegraph Avenue and completed my search in the market. As I walked out the sliding doors, I was startled by the sudden entry of an ancient Datsun pickup into the store's small parking lot, where it skidded to a stop in front of me. I saw a young man behind the windshield of the truck, frozen with fear. He was being pursued closely by a police cruiser, lights flashing.

In an instant, two law enforcement officers were out of their vehicle and at each side of the truck. One of them had pulled out a nightstick and tapped sharply on the driver's side window. "Turn off the engine and put your hands on the wheel, or I will CRACK . . . YOUR . . . SKULL," he informed the driver with extreme conviction and clarity. The officer then glanced at me; I was glued to the pavement in front of the trunk, clutching my purchase and staring with wide eyes. "Get the fuck out of here," he instructed. I nodded once and immediately retreated down Parker Street towards our house.

The trouble had started earlier in the week when the university, which formally owned People's Park, had begun the installation of volleyball courts on its southern edge, with plans to further develop it into a community playground and surrounding university housing. The reaction from many long-time locals was swift and negative. The history of confrontation between the town, the university, and law enforcement over the tiny parcel of real estate stretched back for over a generation. The university had been trying to develop the site in fits and starts since the late 1950s, but after repeatedly running short on cash, commitment, and a definitive plan of action, had allowed it to sit derelict until the spring of 1969. By that point, activists had claimed it for themselves as an open space, public park, and free-speech venue outside of the university campus.

The resulting stalemate between the university and community activists ultimately attracted the attention of Governor Ronald Reagan, who had taken to describing Berkeley in his political speeches as "a haven for communist sympathizers, protesters, and sex deviants." At 4:30 a.m. one morning, state and local law enforcement were sent into Berkeley, where they seized an eight-block perimeter around the park and presided over the installation of a fence ten feet tall to prevent any further activities within its boundaries by local citizens.

The resulting protests and confrontations, which had been percolating for the previous month, immediately exploded into violence. By the end of that day, known since as Bloody Thursday, police armed with shotguns had fired at protestors and bystanders on the roofs of neighboring buildings. One young man, James Rector, would not survive his injuries. When physicians who had operated on him provided samples of the buckshot that they had removed from his body, the sheriff of Alameda County defended the use of force, arguing that anything less would have resulted in the abandonment of Berkeley to a mob. He would later concede that his deputies (some of whom were Vietnam combat veterans) may have been overzealous in their pursuit of the demonstrators, treating them "as if they were Viet Cong."

Since those troubled days, the area had continued to operate as an unregulated open space and was viewed by some as a sanctuary for the town's homeless population and an enjoyable location for informal recreational activities, and by others as a dangerous focal point for drug use and criminal behavior. Now, history was repeating itself, as the university again tried to assert its ownership of the park, this time with a plan to build a sports court within its borders. Earlier that day, hundreds of people had assembled at the park, where they were confronted by police in riot gear.

Over the ensuing hours, dozens of protestors were arrested both individually and in groups. Some attempted to play a sarcastic form of volleyball over police lines; many eventually gathered near the chain-link fence surrounding the site of disagreement, ignoring police commands to disperse. Down the street, windows that had been broken in the previous night's protests were boarded up, and an overturned dumpster and its contents had been set ablaze in the middle of the street. Building upon the already tense situation, additional youth from around the area were arriving in Berkeley on the BART system, keen to find an opportunity to throw a rock or bottle at a law enforcement officer.

After my hasty retreat home, I described what I had witnessed just up the street. Nothing I had experienced during in my years in the northwest or northeast corners of the country had informed me that riots were still happening in the USA. I naively associated them with news footage and documentaries from the 1960s and the civil rights era. Within an hour, we were watching from our front doorstep as crowds of demonstrators, augmented by individuals with less noble goals than the preservation of an open space, were herded down Parker Street by a phalanx of motorcycle police and foot patrol officers. Those that turned to face the police were greeted by rounds of beanbags and rubber bullets fired at them by the advancing lines of law enforcement. After watching two young men knocked off their feet by the projectiles (one of whom, hit square in the mouth, would clearly be needing dental surgery in his near future), we retreated into our house, locked the door, and turned out the lights.

That week in Berkeley would not only educate me in how quickly political and social conflict could spiral into violence and chaos, it would also serve as the starting line for five of the most eventful months of my life, culminating in my second trip to the Soviet Union with Payload Systems. The only complication would be that by the time we finally arrived in Moscow, the Soviet Union would no longer exist.

The pace of my research activities in the Koshland lab, and of my travels, picked up significantly in the fall of 1991. I had unexpectedly found myself leaving town for faculty interviews, as well as for meetings with Payload Systems to begin the planning process for our next mission to Baikonur. Earlier that summer, I had noticed an advertisement in the back pages of the journal *Science* from the Fred Hutchinson Cancer Research Center in Seattle. Their posting indicated that they were in the earliest stages of creating a research program in structural biology and protein crystallography and were inviting applications from interested postdoctoral research fellows.

The advertisement immediately caught my eye; the chance to return to the Pacific Northwest and start my own lab was an enticement I could not overlook. I had quickly written up a description of my research interests and potential plans for my own lab and sent it off to Seattle. Having done so, I noticed several similar advertisements from other academic institutions around the country and had applied to them as well. Now, I was starting to hear back from them, and was surprised to find myself being invited to travel to their campuses to present my work and interview with their faculty. The first trip, scheduled in mid-October, would be in Seattle itself.

By August, I had been informed by Payload Systems that they had in fact successfully negotiated a paid sponsorship and partnership for the next mission with Fujitsu Inc., as well as a second partnership with the Canadian Research Council. Each of those organizations would be providing cash, along with protein crystallization samples for our next set of experiments that would join additional experiments that Roland, Greg, and I were providing.

We met with Anthony and Payload's engineers to discuss and plan for the mission. In addition to the experiments being provided by our sponsors, all three of us had new proteins and crystallization problems that we were planning to include in the second mission. In the days preceding our arrival in Moscow, Roland and I would be responsible for traveling to the laboratories of our industrial and governmental research partners to pick up their samples and would then arrive and meet in Russia from opposite directions. I would be traveling back to Tokyo for that purpose, and then farther westward to Moscow, while Roland would be traveling from Canada with a newly hired engineer at Payload Systems named Chris Krebs. Greg would remain in the States; he had found his first and only Russian experience a year earlier to be entirely sufficient to satisfy his wanderlust and curiosity.

By the end of our final meeting, Roland and I had agreed on three non-negotiable points for the next trip. The first was that both of us would independently travel with a supply of rubber seals sufficient to assemble our devices several times over. The second was that the two of us would provide considerable input into the contents of the "extra shipping" case that was packed for the trip, making sure it contained sufficient non-perishable food items to reduce our dependency on beets and horse meat during our stay. I would personally build upon that policy by jamming a variety of additional edible supplies into every extra nook and cranny of my own suitcase.

The third and final expectation, which I would eventually enforce rigidly, was that when the inevitable evening of booze and bonding with our Russian hosts arrived, Roland—rather than me— would step into the line of fire and take one for the team.

Things had not been going well for the Soviet power structure since our departure from Moscow on Christmas Eve nineteen months earlier. Over the course of the following year, the Baltic States of Estonia, Latvia, and Lithuania, along with Armenia, had all declared independence; subsequent attempts by the Soviets to bring them back under control had been violent but unsuccessful. Within Russia itself, local leaders were pushing for an end to Soviet-style political control, and the economic situation had grown desperate, with hyperinflation and shortages of essential goods, services, and fuel reaching a critical point as fall and winter approached.

On August 17, 1991, only two days after my encounter with local protestors and law enforcement on the streets of Berkeley, headlines around the world reported that hardline Soviet leaders had declared a state of emergency in the Soviet Union and were attempting to seize power from Gorbachev. One of them, Gennady Yanayev, had declared himself to be acting Soviet president, claiming that Gorbachev was being replaced due to illness.

Within two days, thousands of Russian troops had taken up positions in Moscow, and local radio and television stations were taken off the air or forced to broadcast declarations of the takeover. Unfortunately for the conspirators, a grave miscalculation would prove disastrous to their coup attempt; they had failed to also take the Russian politician and leader Boris Yeltsin into custody. In less than a week, their ill-fated coup d'état collapsed when the military forces that were charged with attacking the Russian White House (where Yeltsin and his followers were located) refused to follow their orders and instead declared their support of an independent Russian state.

Throughout the final months of 1991, the disintegration of the Soviet Empire continued. Although Mikhail Gorbachev had been reinstated as its leader, his authority was severely limited. Shortly after the coup attempt, Ukraine had declared its independence; within days the Supreme Soviet had suspended all Communist Party activity, essentially dissolving it as a center of political power and organization. Over the final four months of the year, ten republics seceded from the Soviet Union, culminating in the signing of the Belovezha Accords, which effectively ended the existence of the Soviet Union and created in its place the Commonwealth of Independent States. As the preamble of the Accords stated, "The USSR, as a subject of international law and a geopolitical reality, is ceasing its existence."

# ANGRY RED SKIES AND
# ABANDONED RED FLAGS

October 19, 1991

**SUNDAY MORNING HAD** dawned hot and breezy in the East Bay, with strong Santa Ana winds (known locally to older generations of Californians as "Devil Winds") blowing through the town from the east, where Berkeley and neighboring Oakland were bordered by the Hayward Hills and a corresponding geographic fault line. A single highway connected our area with the towns to the east of those hills, passing through the Caldecott Tunnel.

I had just returned to the area from my quick trip to Seattle where I had spent two full days interviewing for a faculty position. That morning I had left the house early in the morning with Ben, dropping him off at a local childcare room while I attended a class. Amy was planning to join me later that morning with Zach, who had just turned four months old and was starting to sit up and roll himself over. We had made plans to spend a family day together, most likely at Tilden Park in the hills above the university campus. I had taken notice of the unusual morning heat and strong winds as we walked the few blocks from our house to the childcare room but thought little of it. We were still relatively new to California, and I usually shrugged at patterns of weather in the area that remained foreign to me.

As I emerged from my class shortly before noon, I was met at the front door by Amy and Zach on the sidewalk. Her eyes were wide, and she simply told me to look up. Stepping out from under the building's overhang and dense foliage of a eucalyptus tree, I tilted my head back and gazed at an angry red sky. Unlike a sunset, however, this color extended across the entire visible horizon. As I peered uncertainly past the tree branches, I noticed streams of smoke in the air, as well as small particles of ash being swept along by increasingly strong winds. Amy informed me that she had been working in the kitchen of our house, when she had suddenly noticed that the hardwood floor had taken on a deep reddish hue. She had looked out the sliding glass door that faced our small backyard area and had immediately spotted smoke pouring into the sky along the hilltops to the east, about two miles from our home. Then, she had caught a glimpse of a sudden fireball as a distant house on the horizon exploded into flame. She had grabbed Zach and quickly made her way to me and Ben, finding us almost immediately upon her arrival.

The maelstrom that we watched nervously throughout the rest of the next day and a half became known afterwards as the Oakland Hills Firestorm. The blaze had started the day before in the form of a relatively small grassfire that had broken out in the hills above the Berkeley-Oakland border. Firefighters had arrived promptly that day, and after several hours believed they had fully contained and extinguished the fire, which consumed about five acres of brush and grass. The next morning, it suddenly and furiously reignited from the remaining embers, growing into a conflagration in a matter of minutes that was stoked by dry winds blowing at up to sixty-five miles per hour. With dry fuel available in abundance, within a half hour it had spread to a nearby apartment complex, and then moved on to the top of the densely packed residential neighborhoods of the Berkeley and Oakland hills.

Within another hour, the fire swept through dozens of city blocks, destroying hundreds of homes at a speed and ferocity that was overwhelming. From our vantage point in the upper floor of our house, we could see individual houses catching fire in sequence as if they were matchsticks in a box. We noted that the destruction was moving steadily down the hillsides towards downtown and our own home, driven by the unrelenting wind. I looked at Amy and told her that I could easily picture the fire driving through the city and down to the bay.

We discussed our plan of action, which fundamentally involved being far away from the area well before the fire crossed into the downtown area. Unaware that dozens of homeowners and residents in the hills above us had already been trapped and killed by the rapidly advancing firestorm (probably after engaging in similar calculations to what Amy and I were now discussing), we felt that it would be reasonable to pack up our car for a quick departure, turn it around to point towards an escape route in the direction of the bay, and then adopt a "wait and see" posture. Amy had recently obtained an enormous quantity of free diapers, courtesy of winning a shopping spree at a local store; the bulk of the car's interior was filled with that windfall. Enough space remained to allow the four of us to drive out of town if necessary.

Looking back on that day, with two small children and ourselves depending on good decisions, it is remarkably easy to question our actions, if not our sanity. At the time, however, we were torn between avoiding danger at all costs versus unnecessarily abandoning the house to an uncertain fate. We were renting it from a married couple who had purchased and renovated it while themselves working towards doctoral degrees at the university. They were now working in postdoctoral positions back East. They had befriended us a year earlier, and, knowing that our family would soon be increasing in size, they had offered us occupancy of their house for a substantial discount over what they could have asked otherwise. They were planning to possibly return to the area in a few years to again take residence in their home and had chosen us as their tenants based on their faith that we would take wonderful care of their property. I very much wanted to avoid explaining why I had blithely allowed it to burn to the ground rather than sticking around for a while longer and see to its security. It was clear to me that the immediate threat, as long as the main fire was still at some distance from us, was in the possibility of burning embers, carried by the winds, igniting the structure's roof. Armed with a garden hose, I felt—perhaps with more confidence than I should have had—that it was reasonable to stay on-site for a while and monitor the situation.

We watched the fire move down the hills for the remainder of the day and evening, live from our bedroom window as well as on the television news. Initial attempts to control it were disastrous; winds continued to gust up to seventy miles per hour or more and firetrucks found themselves unable to access the narrow residential roads into the hills. At the fire's peak, homes burned to the ground at a rate of one every eleven seconds; nearly eight hundred homes were destroyed in the first hours of the blaze. Eventually, firefighting teams on the scene often ran out of water as local reservoirs were depleted.

As the day started to turn dark, we came to a decision. We would stay up, keep the radio and TV on, and monitor the progression of the flames. At the top of the downtown Berkeley area, right where the hills met the extended business community and less than a half mile from our house, stood the Claremont Hotel. That enormous structure, opened in 1915 and containing hundreds of guest rooms, stood as a sentinel over the city. If it caught on fire, we decided, we would immediately abandon the area and hit the road, under the assumption that the whole town would likely burn down.

As the entire region watched on TV, the fire marched down to the edge of the hotel's grounds, advancing one house at a time. Then, as all seemed lost, the winds abruptly died down. The raging fire was finally contained only hundreds of feet from the hotel, although it would not be declared to be fully extinguished for three more days. In the end, 2,843 houses, 437 apartments and condominiums, and twenty-five lives were lost.

After my interview trip to Seattle and subsequent brush with urban wildfire, my schedule loosened, allowing me to concentrate on research in the lab. A funeral was held for a university undergraduate who had been killed in the fire, and controversy over People's Park continued to percolate, although without the level of confrontation we had witnessed firsthand in August. Finally, December took me to New York City, where I joined a group of postdoctoral fellows (who were all being funded for their research by the Helen Hay Whitney Foundation) for a weekend meeting. We traveled by bus from the campus of Rockefeller University on the east side of Manhattan to the Arden House and conference center in the Hudson River Valley. The centerpiece of the facility was the former mansion of railroad magnate E. H. Harriman, sitting on thousands of acres of forest on a low-rising mountaintop east of Harriman Village. Housing ninety-seven guest rooms, it was ideal for meetings.

Four days after my return from New York and two years after our departure from the Soviet Union at the end of our first mission, on Christmas Day of 1991, Mikhail Gorbachev went on Soviet television and resigned as the president of the USSR, stating, "I hereby discontinue my activities at the post of president of the Union of Soviet Socialist Republics." He declared his political office to be nonexistent and transferred his powers as the leader of the Russian people and country to Boris Yeltsin. In its final session later that evening, the Supreme Soviet voted the USSR out of existence. That night, the hammer and sickle were lowered from the Kremlin towers for the final time, and the tricolored flag of Russia was raised in their place.

Early the following month, I would again board a plane and start the longest journey of my life, circumnavigating the globe (and then some) as I regrouped with Roland, Payload Systems, and the Russian Space Agency to again place crystallization experiments on *Mir*. When we arrived in Moscow, we found a new regime in control, a very different atmosphere on the streets of Moscow, and the rapid and unruly introduction of Western-style capitalism already in progress. What remained was the Russian space program, which would now have to deliver our experiments and hardware to *Mir* while simultaneously figuring out how to operate under vastly different rules than it had ever previously experienced.

# KIND OF THE SAME, ONLY
# DIFFERENT AND MUCH WORSE

14 January 1992

**DEAR AMY,**

Hello from Moscow!! It's incredibly COLD here—about 20 below zero with a stiff wind on top of it. Roland, Chris, and I went to Red Square yesterday and saw Lenin, and then went in the Kremlin and toured the churches and museums. I saw relics of Russian history that are unbelievable.

I miss you all very much. See you soon....

My return to Moscow and my personal mission to enter Red Square and the Kremlin's museums differed greatly from my travels in December of 1989. After my first experience in the city, when I had strolled its streets overdressed in an attention-grabbing, all-American parka, I had decided to dress down and thereby blend in more readily with the Moscow citizenry, at the cost of lowering my defenses against the legendary, but apparently overblown Russian winter weather. For that purpose, I had chosen a nondescript flannel wool jacket that I had purchased at a used-clothing store in Cambridge, augmented with a grey sweatshirt underneath for some extra warmth.

Walking out the door of our hotel that morning, I realized I had grievously miscalculated; the two thin layers of outerwear I was wearing were no match for the blast of sub-zero Siberian air and wind that had descended on the capital city. Visions of Napoleon's and Hitler's armies freezing to death during their Russian campaigns came to mind as I made my frigid way down Moscow's broad boulevards and sidewalks towards the Kremlin.

Four days earlier I had packed for an extended trip around the world that would last for the better part of a month. Whereas in the first mission we had sent three research scientists to set up a limited number of experiments involving only two proteins, this time only Roland and I would be setting up crystallization experiments for nineteen separate proteins that had been collected from research laboratories across North America, as well as several additional proteins being provided by Fujitsu. My trip would therefore start with a return to Tokyo to collect their protein samples, before flying on to Moscow. Payload Systems, remembering the drama that had accompanied my exit from Russia at the end of the first mission, had decided to assign an extra person to babysit me during my travels to Japan and onward to Moscow. They had chosen Payload's newly hired project manager, Maria Douglass, for that task. Fluent in Russian, Maria had obtained an undergraduate degree in Soviet Studies and had then jumped into graduate studies focusing on science and technology and business management. For the remainder of our time together, she would serve both as our translator and as our group leader as we negotiated a very new and quite different political and business landscape. First, however, she was given the responsibility of keeping me in line, on task, and out of trouble as we flew around the world.

Early on the morning of Friday, January 10, I made my way to San Francisco International Airport and found her at the ticket counter for our flight to Tokyo on Japan Airlines. While we waited at the gate, I began to tell her stories of my trip to Tokyo one year before, including the virtually non-existent boundary between smoking and non-smoking cabins for the ten-hour flight. She looked at me with amused eyes, and then told me her own favorite story of a past trip that she had taken to Tokyo in the early 1980s. For her return flight, she had been upgraded at the last moment by her employer to the first-class cabin on the 747 airliner, located up a set of stairs above the main cabin. The airline staff had seemed reluctant to show her to her seat, for reasons that became apparent when partway through the flight they began to show adult movies to the group of otherwise entirely male Japanese travelers, while serving them cigars and whiskey.

Upon arrival in Tokyo, we checked in to our hotel for a two-night stay that would bookend a day trip to Fujitsu to collect their protein samples and crystallization reagents for the experiment. Unlike my first trip, we did not have to endure the Tokyo subway system and its mass packaging of human cargo into the train cars; the company provided a driver for the day. This time, I was traveling without crystallization hardware, as it had been separately packed in Cambridge and was making its way around the opposite side of the world. True to the pact that I had made with Roland, however, I was traveling with a package of spare O-rings that I had procured during my last trip to Payload Systems and had carefully stored in my luggage.

The trip to the company's research labs consumed most of the day, starting with a combination of extended pleasantries and conversation when we first arrived, followed by a tour of the laboratory and then an extended hands-on tutorial demonstrating exactly how the Japanese investigators wished for us to mix and load the protein and crystallization buffers into the devices. For their samples, the protocols would be quite different from our typical crystallization experiments, with the solutions being mixed inside our devices right when they were loaded, well before launch and delivery to the space station.

By midafternoon, the company's researchers were satisfied that I understood their proposed experimental setup. Their confidence had seemed to increase when they noted that Maria was paying close attention to our conversations and taking notes as they reiterated their procedures. They appeared to assume that this time I was traveling with a laboratory assistant, and I said nothing to dissuade them. Finally, they informed us that they were ready to hand off their protein samples, for which I would sign and then keep on my person throughout the remainder of our travel to Moscow and Baikonur. A young technician left the laboratory for a few minutes, and then returned with a well-used, bright pink aluminum thermos decorated with flower decals. The thermos had obviously logged many miles and was visibly scarred and dented from what appeared to be years of service to its prior owners. I stared at it momentarily, then looked up at my counterpart, puzzled.

Unscrewing its lid, I peered inside and saw that its interior was packed with crushed ice, into which several sealed tubes of invaluable protein solutions had been inserted. I smiled to myself. I was not sure how much the company was paying for the privilege of flying their own experiments as part of our mission, but I was certain it was not an inexpensive proposition. On top of that cost were the manpower and time that had been spent on generating what were undoubtedly precious amounts of their purified proteins to be used in their drug development research program. The fruit of their labors was now being entrusted to a young American that they had met twice, for a total of less than eight hours, in a thermos bottle that might have originally been part of a Hello Kitty lunchbox set.

As I prepared to leave, I politely asked if they wished to have the thermos returned to them. My question induced a round of rapid-fire dialogue among the researchers in their native tongue; clearly, they had not considered that point. Finally, our host turned, bowed slightly, and informed me that the thermos could be considered a gift and memento of our partnership. To the best of my knowledge, that thermos remains buried somewhere in Payload System's inventory to this very day.

The next morning, the same driver picked us up at our hotel for a final drive to Narita International Airport. We were joined by a company representative, who ushered us through the airport security and to our departure lounge. For this leg of the journey, Maria and I would get to enjoy first-class seats and treatment—all courtesy of the pink thermos and its contents, which Fujitsu had decided should not be subjected to the rigors of traveling coach class. I did nothing to persuade our hosts otherwise and was glad to have the upgrade for the next leg of our journey, which would cover another seven time zones, mostly within Russian airspace. As we followed our escort through the airport, I was surprised to find that we had been cleared to enter its secure zone without passing through a security checkpoint or having ourselves or our belongings searched or scanned. Instead, we were led through a secret passageway and directly into the first-class lounge of Japan Airlines. I could not picture any scenario in which security checkpoints in an American airport could be similarly avoided.

As we prepared to board the flight, Maria asked me if I had used the restroom in the lounge. Puzzled by her question, I responded in the negative and asked why she wished to know. She smiled and informed me that it was outfitted with heated cushioned seats on the toilets, which were an unheard-of novelty to both of us in 1992. I pondered her observation for a moment, and then informed her that I very much wished she had disclosed that information to me earlier. Where we were headed, not only would there be no heated toilet seats, there might very well be no toilet seats at all.

The flight westward consumed the entire day and was remarkable in that the airliner, rather than cruising at a normal altitude of over 30,000 feet, remained instead at about 10,000 feet, thereby providing a mesmerizing, closeup view of the Russian landscape. I recalled that nine years earlier, a Korean Airline flight had been shot down by Soviet air defense after straying into Russian airspace; I assumed that our lower altitude and slower cruising speed were both requirements imposed to make commercial flights easier to monitor. I eventually turned my attention from the window by my seat to the flight's single movie selection, being broadcast throughout the cabin. The soundtrack was offered in four different overdubbed languages, but not in its original English. I fell asleep watching *Robin Hood: Men in Tights* in poorly synchronized Japanese.

Upon landing at Sheremetyevo, we were again met by Payload Systems Engineers. They were accompanied by Roland, who was looking somewhat ragged; he always struggled mightily with sleep deprivation and jet lag when he was traveling, usually accompanied by the immediate development of cold symptoms. As we drove downtown, he told me about his travels thus far, and the events in Moscow since his arrival twenty-four hours earlier. He and his travel companions from Payload had been joined by an elderly scientific representative from the National Research Council of Canada, which had provided both funding and proteins from several of the Canadian crystallography laboratories that were supported by that agency. Roland had immediately taken a strong disliking to the man; within a day I would join him in that opinion.

He then went on to tell me about the previous evening's dinner with hosts from the Russian Space Agency. They had been joined by several military officials, one of whom was a commanding officer at the Baikonur facility and would be traveling with us back to Kazakhstan. As dinners and receptions in Russia tend to go, this one had been quite tame, but nonetheless shots and toasts of vodka had been forthcoming and unavoidable. Roland had gamely joined in, at one point standing to offer a toast to the newly formed Confederation of Independent States. As soon as his well wishes were translated, he could see that he had miscalculated; the Russian officer's eyes narrowed, as he scowled. Setting his glass down forcefully, he had fixed Roland with a cold stare and then announced, in perfect English, "We will be back."

Apart from my friend creating a minor diplomatic incident, the start of our mission otherwise appeared to be moving forward without issue. All the equipment had arrived intact, and like me, Roland had brought his own extra package of O-rings along with the remaining protein samples. He informed me that I would find the hotel to be a pleasant surprise. As we pulled up, I gazed at the entrance to the Radisson Slavyanskaya, where we would stay both before and after our journey to Baikonur. The hotel had opened after extensive renovations the previous July, only a few months before the final fall of the Soviet Union—the first of many American-managed chain hotels that would infiltrate the city as communism was replaced by its successor.

A news article published in the *New York Times* about the development, shortly after the hotel's opening, had pulled no punches in quoting the founder and chairman of the managing company. "The quality of most Russian hotels is abysmal, in Mr. Carlson's opinion, because under the former Soviet ownership there was no incentive to upgrade or even maintain the existing quality. 'They built the hotels and put in the furniture,' he said, 'but they never went back and replaced things.'" In contrast, we were delighted to find our rooms to be appointed with Western-quality mattresses, bedding, and climate control; I slept more soundly than during any of the nights that I had spent in the Soviet bloc in 1989.

Unlike our prior trip, we were provided with a free day in Moscow to help our internal clocks adjust to the time zone change before departing to Baikonur. I was glad for the short respite; this time we were scheduled to spend eleven days in Baikonur, rather than the five that had been required to set up far fewer experiments in mission one. While life in Moscow had gotten easier for traveling American scientists and engineers since our last visit, I was sure that the comfort level in Baikonur would not be improved to any significant extent. Even that minimal expectation would quickly be squashed after our arrival—it would actually prove to be much, much worse.

Chris, Roland, and I decided to spend our free day accomplishing what had proven to be impossible in December of 1991, by walking to Red Square and touring its grounds and museums. Unlike our previous trip, the city was devoid of troops and barriers, a clear indication that the conflict that had accompanied the fall of communism had subsided. Not only were the streets clear of military forces, but they were also largely devoid of people altogether. It took only a few moments outdoors to understand why; it was brutally cold, far below zero degrees with a stiff wind blowing as we left our hotel shortly after breakfast.

I would later find out, after consulting with the front desk, that we had stepped out into a winter temperature of -20°F that morning (plus wind chill), eventually warming up to a balmy six degrees. Nonetheless, we were determined to see the sites, so we resolutely marched down Arbat Street towards Red Square. Whereas Roland was wearing a thick jacket and had invested in the largest Russian fur-lined hat he could find, I had no covering other than the hood of my sweatshirt extending from under my thin wool jacket. I wrapped it around my head and ears tightly.

By the time we reached Red Square, my eyes were streaming and my head pounding from the cold. No matter which way I turned, the unrelenting wind seemed to blow directly into my face. Eventually, I sought refuge behind the east Kremlin Wall. The entire area extending along the wall was a burial ground and necropolis, flanked by a nearby granite structure that housed Lenin's corpse. Directly in front of me, individual obelisks with head-and-shoulder sculptures on top marked the burial sites of six of the most notorious and murderous of past Russian leaders: Mikhail Suslov, Mikhail Kalinin, Felix Dzerzhinsky,

Leonid Brezhnev, Yuri Andropov, and Joseph Stalin.

Of the six, Stalin's tomb was conspicuously covered with flowers and ribbons recently left by Moscow residents. It was clear to me that much of the city's population, faced with the uncertainty left by the collapse of the old order, wished for the return of a strong man like the despot who had adopted the surname "Steel." I briefly pondered the countless number of lives that had been destroyed by the whims, paranoia, thirst for power, and bloodlust of the individuals entombed in front of me, and then moved on.

Our flight to Baikonur was uneventful, differing from two years earlier only in that we would land in the newly independent country of Kazakhstan, rather than the Soviet Republic of Kazakhstan. After showing our travel credentials to an official of what I assumed was a hastily created customs and immigration department, we gathered our belongings and crates of laboratory equipment and boarded our vans. My battered pink thermos, which had aroused considerable curiosity when we passed through airport security, and my personal supply of O-rings were kept closely guarded on my person. Departing from the airport, we drove past the neighboring town and our prior hotel, and then immediately turned onto the long road towards the Baikonur launch facility. I turned toward my travel companions with a confused look; it was getting late in the afternoon, and I had assumed we would be heading straight towards our lodging for the evening. Surely, we weren't going to be unloading and setting up the lab at this late hour? We had numerous days in front of us to complete our work, so I doubted there was any urgency.

Maria noticed my questioning look and provided her best effort at a reassuring smile. Things were going to be different on this trip, she explained. While the launch facility and its grounds remained under Russian control, they were now being rented from Kazakhstan, which had quickly mastered the essential concept of supply and demand that fuels capitalism. The surrounding area and its facilities, as well at the utilities that powered, fueled, and hydrated the base, were under Kazak control and subject to whatever pricing they decided to demand of their Russian guests. Apparently, the quoted rate for a stay at the hotel facility in the neighboring town was more than the Russians or Payload Systems were willing to pay. Therefore, we would all be staying in a section of barracks at the launch site itself, lodging that was normally occupied by troops living on the base.

I sat back in my seat and pondered this news, which apparently had also been a surprise to the advance team that had preceded our arrival. Given that the final dissolution of the Soviet Union and formation of the newly independent state of Kazakhstan had occurred only three weeks earlier, it should not have been surprising that even simple issues such as lodging were in disarray. Nonetheless, the speed with which the new country and its local governmental officials had grasped the economic situation and then decided to try to screw their former Russian bosses was impressive. *No matter how the impending change in scenery plays out,* I thought, *I doubt it will work to our benefit.*

Upon arrival at the facility, we unloaded our crates and baggage. Our first stop was the cosmodrome itself, where we were reintroduced to the cosmonaut dressing room and adjoining meeting area where we had worked so diligently during the first mission to set up the lab and assemble the flight hardware. To my eyes, it looked as if the chairs and tables had not been touched since our departure. After dropping off our cases of laboratory equipment, we were then escorted out of the building and across the compound to a nondescript single-story structure that resembled a shotgun shack expanded to the size of a very small dormitory. Several Russian soldiers eyed us coldly as we carried our suitcases, backpacks, and a pink thermos across the frozen ground to our quarters. I wondered if they had been forced from their living space and ordered to hot bunk together elsewhere on the base to make room for us.

Each of us was assigned a room; Roland and I were next door to one another. I entered mine and assessed my home for the next week and a half—a single room, about ten feet on each side, containing a well-worn cot, a small rudimentary desk, an ancient electric space heater plugged into the wall, and a large toilet sitting within feet of the bed and separated from it by a thin divider. A small dirty window faced the compound outside. In the middle of the room sat a large, galvanized steel bucket, containing about three gallons of water. I gazed at it for a moment, not sure of its purpose, but sensing intuitively that it was probably a harbinger of future anxiety. I set down my suitcase, backed out of the room, and checked in with Roland. His room was similarly equipped, and his own bucket of water was similarly positioned. We quietly conferred with one another, and then decided to ask some questions.

We went straight to Maria, assuming that her skills in the Russian language might be useful. We found her engaged in quiet conversation with one our hosts from the space agency. As their dialogue continued and then concluded, her eyes widened considerably. Then she turned to us and explained the situation. The newfound understanding and embrace of capitalism by the freshly formed Kazakhstan government and its local officials extended well beyond the nightly rates at town hotel; they were also asking for and expecting exorbitant payments for delivery of basic utilities to the isolated military base and launch facility, including electricity and water. In response the Russians had dug in their heels, refused to pay, and were flying in daily deliveries of water and fuel for electric generators. The buckets in our rooms, she continued, contained our sole source of water for all personal needs during our stay and would be replenished one time each morning. "And" she helpfully added, "that includes flushing your toilet."

I retreated to my room, sat slowly on the edge of my cot, and considered the situation carefully. Then, as the implications of this new information solidified in my mind, I examined the commode more closely. It was an old Russian contraption and was currently bone dry; I was certain it would require a substantial volume of water to flush and clear the bowl. With overwhelming conviction and complete clarity of purpose, I decided that for the remainder of my time in Kazakhstan, the daily allotment of water would be devoted, in its entirety if necessary, to keeping the toilet properly functioning and presentable. Bathing and any other matters of personal hygiene could wait until we returned to the motherland.

We reported for a group dinner with our hosts back in the same building where we would start setting up the lab the next day. The meeting room outside of our workspace was where we ate our meals, which were prepared in an adjoining military kitchen. While I had steeled myself for the renewed daily consumption of beets, I was unprepared for an onslaught of dishes featuring the disgusting root. (Weeks after our return from the trip, the fax machine back in our lab in Berkeley would spring to life and spit out a single page sent to me from Chris Krebs, featuring a *Far Side* cartoon alluding to a fictional "Age of Beets." Across it, Chris had written, with a bold felt-tipped pen, "Lest we ever forget.")

The next morning was devoted to setup of the lab as before. We had many more devices to assemble, to accommodate twenty-one different protein samples from academic and corporate laboratories and had two new individuals helping to do so. The first was Chris; we put him to work with little effort or concern, knowing that his training as an engineer and familiarity with the hardware would be adequate to assure the quality of his work. The second was the representative from the Canadian Research Council, who was insistent he should be directly involved in all steps involving Canadian research samples. Roland, who on his best day in Kazakhstan was far less than affable, had not yet moderated in his obvious, visible disdain for the man. I tried to be more open-minded but found it hard to do so as his first sets of assembled devices leaked mercilessly and required a complete breakdown and reassembly. By the end of the day, we were running behind schedule.

The next two days we continued to systematically assemble and flight-test individual units of crystallization hardware and to reassemble several devices put together by our new colleague. By the end of day three in the lab, we were back on schedule and preparing for the upcoming loading of the primary hardware. Roland and I quietly celebrated our milestone, as well as our surplus of O-rings, as the final devices successfully passed their necessary leak tests and were certified for loading and flight.

Our Russian hosts, with visible satisfaction, received documentation that the primary and backup sets of flight hardware were ready for use. Two years before, they had in fact noticed our short-lived distress in the lab; despite our explanation of paperwork snafus, they had correctly surmised that we had encountered a glitch in our hardware assembly protocols, which fortunately had not become a major issue. That evening, after our fifth straight dinner featuring a beet entrée and bottles of the same Armenian cognac, there were calls for a post-dinner celebration. Roland and I looked knowingly at each other. The night of alcohol-fueled bonding between Russians, Americans, and one annoying Canadian was upon us. Slowly, I raised one hand and pointed two fingers directly at Roland's eyes, silently reminding him of our agreement that he would be the one to step into the line of fire. After three rounds of toasts around the dinner table, I excused myself, explaining that I was feeling a bit under the weather, but that my comrade from Pasadena would be delighted to represent the scientific research team for the remainder of the evening.

I slept very well that night, interrupted only by an extended commotion in the hallway outside my room in the early hours of the morning as the evening's celebrants returned from their time together. I had been fleetingly aware of noise and conversation in Russian occurring on the other side of the wall that I was sharing with Roland, then had rolled over and immediately gone back to sleep.

The next morning at breakfast Roland was late to arrive. When he did, I examined him as he cautiously made his way to a spot at the table that I had left open for him. He was clearly a shattered version of his normal self; his usual pale complexion had lightened into the appearance of a several days-old corpse. His eyes now resided in two dark, sunken pits. Adding to the effect, five days without bathing had mottled and plastered his hair to his head, creating the impression of a skull cap comprised of greasy human hair. (In contrast, the same number of days without a shower or shampoo had exactly the opposite effect on me. My own hair was standing on end and extending from my scalp such that it appeared I was being electrocuted.)

I scrutinized him as he sat and stared unhappily at his plate of food. He was clearly not yet in the mood for chatting, and in any case, he did not appear capable of putting together a truly coherent thought. I left him alone in his suffering and excused myself, after first pouring him a cup of coffee. I met up with Chris in our lab space, where we would start to load protein samples without Roland's immediate participation. Chris had also been involved in the evening's drinking session but was in a much more functional and communicative state. He joined me as we started the slow deliberate process of dispensing protein and crystallization solutions into the individual wells of the first devices and documenting each experimental condition.

Roland joined us within the hour, and to his credit and my surprise was able to participate in the work, albeit largely in autopilot mode. By late morning the fog had started to lift, and he was able to respond to simple phrases and questions. Later that day, during a midafternoon break, I asked him what he remembered about the night before. Unlike my experience, where the details of the final hours of the toasting session had been lost to an alcohol-fueled blackout, Roland remembered it all and was struggling to process his experience. He told us that at the very end of the last round of toasts and shots he had felt his ability to remain upright, as well as his ability to talk or otherwise communicate, slip away, and he ultimately found himself lying silently on the floor.

After a short consultation among the Russians, which included the same commanding officer whom he had unintentionally insulted in Moscow a week earlier, they carried him back to his room and deposited him on his bed. Roland was still fully conscious and cognizant of the actions surrounding him but was unable to speak, looking at his hosts with unblinking eyes. They carefully undressed him to his boxers and positioned his head on a pillow so that he might sleep things off. However, before they left, they engaged in a final conversation in Russian, obviously concerned about his state. Then, as he continued to stare at them helplessly, the officer opened a bottle of mineral water, poured a small amount on his bare chest, and rubbed it around on his exposed skin. They then covered him with a blanket, quietly bade him a good night's sleep, and departed for their own rooms.

To this day, Roland and I occasionally wonder if the gentle application of mineral water directly to the torso is a time-honored Russian method to ease a person through the final stages of an extended drinking session and usher him into the first stages of a subsequent recovery process, or if they were just fucking with him.

At the end of the next day, the Russians surprised us with an offer to transport us into the town so that we could use the showers in the local hotel where we had stayed two years earlier. Given that we had not bathed in a week, we readily accepted, and within the hour we were traveling down the-two lane road, bathroom kits in hand. Roland was especially grateful; two nights before he had tried to suspend his water bucket above his space heater in an ill-fated attempt to warm its contents slightly for a morning wash-up, only to have his contraption collapse in the middle of the night and short-circuit his sole source of warmth. We were both extremely grateful that he had not burned down the barracks.

The Russians looked no less eager to bathe than we did; clearly everyone had reached the limits of their tolerance for personal filth and the stench of unwashed engineers, scientists, and staff members. Walking into the hotel, we passed the sauna and dipping pool on our way to the nearby communal showers. I examined the scene of the crime from the first mission, wondering exactly where on the tile floor I had landed two years earlier, at the end of my own evening with our hosts.

Two days later, we had completed loading all the flight hardware and transferred the primary set to Russian officials for loading into the Soyuz capsule. After we packed up the lab, we were approached by a representative from NPO Energia, the Russian agency in charge of the actual administration of the launch site and space station. They had something special to show us, they declared. Would we be so kind as to accompany them to a nearby building? We nodded assent and made a short walk across the facility to an enormous nearby building. We had noted the facility throughout our prior trip and current time at the cosmodrome but had never asked its contents or purpose. As we walked into the building through a small side door, we looked ahead, and then stopped and gasped in unison.

In front of us stood the Russians' own version of a space shuttle, known as the Buran spaceplane, in an otherwise unoccupied hangar. The enormous vehicle was uncannily similar in appearance to

NASA's own space shuttles and rose several stories over our heads. Although those in the space industry knew about the existence of Buran, it had been largely kept from the public eye, having flown a single, automated non-crewed flight in 1988. Since then, it had been locked away in this remote location, awaiting the moment of its next test flight. Now, however, the sudden loss of the Soviet Union made for a very unclear and unlikely future. If they couldn't pay for water, it seemed highly unlikely that the Russian space program would find a way to continue developing and flying the monstrous space craft.

Our host allowed us to walk around the shuttle, gazing up at its cockpit far above our heads, and then climb stairs to an elevated walkway to view its profile from above. As we descended back to the floor level and began thanking him for the tour, he eyed us with a slight smile. Then he held up a finger. "Would you like," he asked, "to take a piece of Buran home with you as a souvenir?" For fifty US dollars, he explained, we could buy a flight-used, heat-absorbing tile from its surface. "We'll even mount a model of a Progress rocket on it."

We looked at each other for a brief moment. Then, we all started digging frantically into our wallets to see how much cash we had on hand. Fortunately, Chris and Maria had come loaded with US currency (in addition to the case of cigarettes, alcohol, and jeans) for whatever contingency might arise requiring American cash or bartering tools. Soon, we were all walking out of the hangar with a small piece of Buran—testimony to both the best-laid plans of the Soviet space program and to the disintegration of those hopes along with the government that had put them into action. That souvenir remains on a shelf in my office to this very day.

Launch was scheduled for 7:50 a.m. the next day, January 25. The morning dawned crystal clear and extremely cold. As we rode in vans to the same observation post as two years before, I gazed out at the surrounding hills and fields, and at the rocket at its launch site. Over a mile away, the rocket seemed so distant, relative to the energy and noise that I knew we would soon experience. We gathered on the platform as a group, shivering as we waited. Then, only a few seconds after 7:50 a.m., the Progress M11 spacecraft lifted off. It was the first such spacecraft sent to *Mir* following the dissolution of the Soviet Union and was the twenty-ninth of sixty-four such unmanned rockets that would eventually be sent to the space station. As before, the roar and vibration of the rocket as it cleared the launch pad was astonishing in its immediacy and power. However, this time we were able to take pictures as the rocket sped off. The acceleration was incredible; in the amount of time that I required to snap three pictures, quickly advancing the film between each, the rocket was gone.

Unlike our weather-induced detention after the launch in December 1989, this time the clear skies meant that we could leave immediately to return to Moscow and then home. We wasted no time. The Russians had again scheduled a special military flight to deliver us from Baikonur, and the plane was waiting for us. We returned to the base to gather our baggage and laboratory gear and within an hour were boarding our flight. Soon after, we were in the air. Unlike our previous escape, this time we were joined in the forward cabin by multiple Russian counterparts, who almost immediately began opening bottles and presenting toasts to the launch. Roland and I both participated, while trying to minimize the number of shots that we were offered. Less than an hour into the flight, we noticed that the pilot had left the cockpit and joined us in drinking, leaving the single copilot in control of the plane. Soon, the pilot, clearly happy to chat up an attractive young American woman who spoke his native language fluently, fell into a conversation with Maria. Their interaction eventually led to her being invited to sit in the pilot's seat of the cockpit, where she was encouraged to take the controls under their guidance.

I watched her through the open door as she put on headphones and grasped the yolk, and then glanced at Roland. We both raised our eyebrows as we realized that our translator was being encouraged to fly the plane. She would later inform us that as she had sat in the seat, a call had come in from a flight controller asking her to change her heading to avoid another airliner in the vicinity. With the helpful guidance of the copilot, she had executed a slight turn and increased the cruising altitude of our flight.

Two years later, we were vividly reminded of our experience on that flight back to Moscow, when Aeroflot Flight 593 crashed into the side of a mountain, killing all seventy-five passengers and crew on board. At the controls of the plane in the moments leading up to the crash were the teenage children of one of the pilots.

Our return to Moscow was short and joyful. We checked back into the Radisson Slavyanskaya and immediately enjoyed our second shower in almost two weeks; I remained under the hot water for the better part of a half hour. Then, we were treated to what remains one of the most memorable and satisfying meals that I have ever enjoyed, when sacks of burgers and fries from the first McDonald's in Russia were delivered to our rooms. Roland and I dined together that evening, and in the process learned the proper Cyrillic spelling of cheeseburger and quarter pounder.

The next morning, I returned to Sheremetyevo International Airport and left my companions behind, choosing to return to the States and my family rather than remain for an extra day to view the docking of the Soyuz capsule with *Mir* and subsequent activation of our experiments. Unlike my prior departure, my transit through the Moscow airport was uneventful. Twenty hours later I arrived back in San Francisco, having traveled around the world, plus an extra trip from Moscow to Baikonur and back, in sixteen days. This time, my family was faithfully waiting for me at the gate.

# *MIR* FOR THE MONEY

Is Barry the crystallographer wise?
He has no geographical ties
From Palo Alto to the Russias,
He uses big atom crushas,
And then he tries to energy minimize!
—Dan Koshland, composed and recited on the eve of my
departure from Berkeley

January 28, 1992

**I RETURNED TO** Berkeley at the end of January and found a letter waiting for me from the Hutchinson Center in Seattle that had been written and posted the day before I left for Russia, offering me a faculty position in their newly constructed research campus. Within a short period of time, I completed negotiations for a startup package and salary, and began making plans to leave Berkeley at the end of November to head back to the Pacific Northwest, where I would start the next stage of my career as a faculty member.

Over the next ten months, there was much to do, not least of which was to retrieve the crystallization devices from the ongoing mission on the *Mir* space station and distribute them to the individual labs throughout North America and Japan, whereupon individual teams of crystallographers would document their crystallization results and the performance of the best specimens in front of an X-ray beam. The reentry capsule carrying cosmonauts and our hardware would return to earth in late March; we would meet the experiments back in Cambridge a few days later, collect the devices containing our own experiments, and dispatch Payload Systems employees to deliver the rest to our partners on the mission.

Both before and after, I would have several pressing issues to attend to, including the preparation of a series of manuscripts from my postdoctoral work to date and the design and ordering of a new X-ray laboratory for the Hutchinson Center. I was lost deep in thought as I strolled into the center of campus, then stopped as the warm breeze of the California morning carried the fragrant smell of the surrounding eucalyptus trees. Just a few days earlier, I had been standing in subzero temperatures in Kazakhstan, shivering as I waited to see the launch of a Russian supply rocket carrying the second set of American experiments to the *Mir* space station. Now, I was striding across campus in shorts, a tropical shirt, and a pair of flip-flops, enjoying a beautiful warm morning in Northern California. My momentary revelry was interrupted as a tall young man casually walked past me, naked, carrying nothing on his person but a small pack slung over his shoulder. As I cocked my head and stared with surprise, puzzlement, and a bit of admiration at his tanned backside, it hit me that I was indeed back home in the rather strange place known as Berkeley.

The "naked guy" burst onto the scene on the university campus in early 1992 and quickly became a local phenomenon and then a nationwide topic of conversation. Named Andrew Martinez, the twenty-year-old upperclassman had suddenly decided to walk the campus and attend classes wearing nothing more than a G-string, but only upon request. He had decided to do so, he told those who asked, to make a statement regarding the right to personal freedom of choice. Naturally, his actions caught the attention of local law enforcement (who eventually decided that in the absence of actual lewd behavior, there was no obvious law being broken), the local media (who couldn't resist such a juicy story), and the local citizenry (who viewed his actions as unconventional, but not nearly as strange as many others that occurred frequently within the borders of the city).

At one point during his reign of nudity, a local theater troupe renamed themselves "the X-Plicit players" and staged a form of performance art on Sproul Plaza in which they shed their own clothing and encouraged onlookers to join them. The festivities were eventually brought to a halt when one particularly ragged homeless man began to disrobe, causing the crowd to become distracted as they collectively encouraged him to please put his clothes back on.

As I watched Naked Guy turn the corner and head towards a cluster of buildings, I concluded that while his actions were certainly provocative, they were not particularly extraordinary when carried out by a tall, muscular, strikingly handsome undergraduate under the warmth of the California sunshine. I would have been vastly more impressed to see a middle-aged businessman in Boston, Moscow, or Kazakhstan make a similar fashion statement in the middle of the winter.

I returned to Cambridge at the end of March, where I joined Greg and Roland for a weekend to meet the flight hardware upon its return from Russia. The units that were loaded with the Japanese proteins had not traveled back to the USA, having instead been transported from Moscow directly back to the laboratory at Fujitsu by a Payload Systems employee. We would never hear the results of their experiments. The three of us took most of the units back to each of our respective laboratories in California and Pennsylvania, where we each photographed the crystals and subjected them to X-ray analysis. The plan was to have all the data documenting the effects of microgravity on their size and performance collected and turned into a short research report by the end of the summer. To our surprise, we had already been contacted by the editors of *Nature* to request that we submit a short article to them summarizing our results and our recommendations for future work.

A month after I returned to Berkeley, it again became an urban war zone, with our house on the edge of considerable violence, mayhem, rioting, and looting. In contrast to the prior confrontation between the university, local Berkeley residents, and police over the development of People's Park, the protests this time—which had rapidly turned deadly—were ignited by the outcome of the trial of four law enforcement officials in Los Angeles. A year earlier, Rodney King had been brutally assaulted by the police officers at the conclusion of a high-speed chase; the beating had been videotaped by a local resident from an apartment balcony and then broadcast on TV. When the not-guilty verdict from the officers' trial was handed down on the afternoon of April 29, it sparked collective outrage that would result in six days of rioting and carnage throughout the LA area, with over sixty deaths, thousands of injuries and fires, and hundreds of millions of dollars in losses to local communities and businesses.

In Berkeley, merchants along Telegraph Avenue began closing early and boarding up their storefronts immediately upon hearing of the verdict. The subsequent riot made the troubles during the prior spring over People's Park seem mild by comparison. At its peak, a fire truck was burned on Telegraph Avenue, additional cars in the area were turned over and torched, and hundreds of arrests were made in one night. Adding to the uprising, individuals from throughout the area descended on Berkeley, not to protest social injustice and police brutality but instead to break into retail businesses while law enforcement was distracted. A writer for *The Daily Cal* would later report that "looters not only came to loot; they brought a shopping list." Dozens of businesses suffered enormous losses and damage; several would never reopen.

By the end of the week, the city had enacted its first and only emergency curfew. That, along with hundreds of police officers placed on the streets and the natural tendency of riots to burn themselves out, eventually restored order. During our remaining months in Berkeley, we lived alongside the remains of abandoned businesses only blocks from our house, as well as racks of stolen merchandise being sold at the weekly Berkeley flea market.

By the beginning of summer, the data collected on the crystallization experiments was largely pulled together, and the three of us were faced with a slight dilemma. Between ourselves and the various Canadian researchers who had participated in the mission, we had sent nineteen separate protein samples, each spanning dozens of crystallization chambers and conditions, into orbit. The results of each were compared not only to parallel experiments set up in duplicate hardware on Earth, but also to the best crystals we could grow in our labs using any method available to us. True to our word when we had first been approached by Payload Systems four years earlier, we were carrying out honest comparisons to judge not only the effect of zero gravity, but the value of zero gravity when compared to the best results that one might expect on Earth (while investing much less effort, time, and cash).

The results were not extremely impressive, but neither were they a total bust. Out of all the experimental systems tested, one out of four exhibited measurable improvement in crystal size and X-ray diffraction performance. The remaining three-fourths of the proteins that we had sent into orbit either showed no improvement or failed to crystallize altogether. We discussed the results with one another. *Nature* was expecting us to send them a report soon, and we were ready to do so. However, the best we could manage would be to state the obvious—sometimes crystallization in space might help, but more often would accomplish relatively little. Then as before, it was difficult to argue that the type of investment and effort in launching crystallization experiments into orbit represented a wise and cost-effective strategy for future studies and drug development efforts.

We knew that we would soon have to provide Payload Systems with our results and a draft of the proposed report. I imagined that they would not be thrilled. Beyond Payload Systems, we also worried about the broader response from NASA and their own cadre of academic crystallographers, who continued to tout the potential of crystals in space as a panacea that would eventually open broad new avenues for biomedical research and development. The prospect of an ongoing argument with multiple established investigators around the country, all supported by NASA, was not attractive.

I decided to chat with Dan about the state of the project and get his thoughts on how to deliver the news to Payload. He was the most experienced scientific statesman and leader I had ever met; if anyone could give sound advice on how to navigate a potential scientific minefield, it would be him. As luck would have it, he was hosting our lab's annual summer barbecue at his home during the upcoming weekend. I looked forward to the gathering; it had been a while since I had visited with him, and I missed our regular interactions and conversations. The last time I had sat in his office, he had regaled me with stories of working on the isolation and characterization of radioactive isotopes during the Manhattan Project, for which he had been pressed into service while studying at the University of Chicago.

At one point, after hearing him describe the cavalier manner with which he and his fellow chemists had handled plutonium when first introduced to it, I asked him if he had ever worried about the long-term health risks of his actions in those earlier times. He looked at me, surprised, as if nobody had ever questioned him on that point before, and after a moment's consideration answered my query. "Nope! We're doing fine. But the beryllium guys . . . they're all dead now."

When we arrived at his home, I paused to marvel at the person who was Dan Koshland. Shortly after our arrival in Berkeley, I had learned that he was part of a well-known family composed of a variety of local civic and business leaders, and that he was descended in part from Levi Strauss and one of the principal heirs to that fortune. Dan was an exceptionally wealthy man (with a net value ranked within the top hundred individuals in the country in a recent issue of *Forbes Magazine*) but cared little about the visible trappings and material accumulations that his family fortune had brought him. Instead, he focused his attention on only two things— his family and his science. Nonetheless, during my first visit to his home the prior summer, I had noticed an original Picasso sketch that hung in the entryway of his house. Otherwise, one would never have imagined that the owner of the house was a person of such means. While it was a lovely home, it was as understated and casual as the man who lived there.

We had arrived a bit late for the party, as getting out the door on time with both a one- and two-year-old child could be challenging on any given morning. By the time we arrived, people were getting hungry, and Dan was predictably overdue to get his charcoal grill fired up. This was a regular part of the annual lab barbecue. Inevitably he would become distracted by conversation and stories and forget his duties as a host, until Marion finally reminded him that he had a backyard full of hungry guests. He would then hurriedly light the charcoal briquets, rapidly growing impatient as they failed to immediately kindle into white-hot coals suitable for cooking. In the next stage of the drama, Dan would produce a can of lighter fluid and begin to spray it directly on the already lit and smoking grill. We would nervously back away from the eminent scientist as he flirted with immolating himself, prepared to throw him into his swimming pool if he accidentally lit himself on fire.

Later that afternoon, I stood by his side with a beer in hand. He sheepishly told me about his latest trip to the East Coast from which he had just returned, and the alarm that he had inadvertently caused to his family and friends as a result. In his role as the senior editor of the journal *Science*, he spent one week each month in the Washington, DC, area, before returning to Berkeley for the remaining three weeks. He had been following that schedule for years, always flying out on a Sunday and returning the following Friday evening. This past trip, however, he had been invited to remain on the East Coast for an extra day and to travel up the road to Baltimore, where he was scheduled to give the keynote address at the annual meeting of the Protein Society on Saturday.

Unfortunately, by the end of the week he had completely forgotten about that obligation. Compounding his mental gaffe, even though he had noted that his normal flight schedule and hotel reservation had been extended by an extra pair of nights, he was unable to remember why. Without a calendar to consult, and with his administrative assistant gone for the weekend, he had decided that he must have desired to take an extra day to be a tourist and had spent his entire free Saturday viewing the museums and monuments in the nation's capital. The lab and his wife, along with several of his friends back in California, had received panicked calls from the meeting organizers when he didn't show up for his talk, leading them to worry that he was lying dead in a ditch somewhere. Upon his return to Berkeley, he and his poor memory had been met with a considerable amount of relief and mirth from his loved ones and colleagues.

I updated Dan on the results of our latest mission and experiments and outlined the manuscript we were writing that would summarize our observations and conclusions. He listened carefully and then furrowed his brow as he visualized the article and its ramifications. He didn't think for long, reaffirming what I already knew to be the case, which was that complete and unbiased honesty, accuracy, and clarity in the description of our results was the only path forward.

To color our results and observations based on worries about their reception in either the structural biology community or the space industry was to invite certain disdain by colleagues.

The article would eventually lay out our results and then offer a conclusion that would challenge many in our field who were working with the space industry:

> We conclude that microgravity acts in much the same manner as any other of the standard additives in crystallization experiments. That is to say that it often has no effect, but when it does, it can be either an improvement or a lessening in the quality of the obtained crystals. Microgravity is not a universal panacea for crystals unsuitable for diffraction experiments . . . [and it] has not yet accomplished any significant breakthrough in protein crystal growth. So far, no protein has been reported to crystallize in microgravity that does not crystallize on Earth.
>
> Measured by the yardstick of routine crystal production, microgravity is not yet a success. Given the difficulty and cost of such experiments, we doubt it will be appropriate for many protein-crystallization problems. The final basis by which to assess its importance and usefulness will be the ability to solve protein structures using crystals which could only be grown in microgravity.

We doubled down on our arguments in a by-line summarizing the article:

> It is nearly ten years since the first attempts were made to grow better protein crystals in the low gravity environment of space. Can the cost of these experiments be justified by the results?

We turned our draft of the article over to Anthony, who was serving as a co-author with us, at the end of the summer for his inspection. We expected that he would react negatively, possibly leading to our swift dismissal from the project. His response was surprising and unambiguous—he found no fault with our evaluation, made no requests for alterations, and agreed to be a coauthor on the manuscript. He went on to inform us that while plans were now in the works for mission number three, which was scheduled to occur in slightly over a year in October of 1993, that he would no longer be involved; he was moving on to a new career opportunity. As I listened to him talk about the state of the project and wish us continued success, I realized that while Anthony might have chosen to work as a businessman in his professional career, he remained a scientist at his core.

The remainder of the fall was spent wrapping up my postdoctoral work and preparing for our move to Seattle. I had already been contacted by a young investigator who would soon complete her own training in protein crystallography and was looking to move to the Northwest and obtain a position as staff scientist. After a single telephone conversation, I had offered her a job which she had rapidly accepted; she would meet me at the Hutchinson Center shortly after the new year and help me start setting up the lab. During our conversation the topic of Payload Systems and our project with the Russian space program had come up. She had read our first article describing the results of the first mission and was curious if the project would continue after my move; if so, she was eager to travel to Russia and Kazakhstan herself. *Be careful what you wish for*, I thought. Then I informed her that it just might be possible to arrange such a trip.

We flew up to Seattle as a family in late October to search for a house. On the outbound flight, we had sat in two pairs: Amy and Ben were located together near the front of the main cabin, while Zach and I were several rows farther back. He was now a highly active sixteen-month-old toddler who had just recently achieved upright posture and corresponding mobility. Unlike his older brother, who had started walking (albeit unsteadily) before his first birthday, Zach had stubbornly refused to walk unassisted until well past his own first birthday, but then had suddenly transitioned to a surprisingly quick running stride. He was a bundle of highly mobile kinetic energy driven by a toddler brain, and this evening he was not responding well to being confined to an airline seat for the two-hour flight from the Bay Area to the Pacific Northwest. By the end of the flight, I had had two consecutive airline meals dumped into my lap, courtesy of his rapid, cobra-like strikes when the airline food had been placed on my seatback tray table.

By the end of November, we had packed up and sent our possessions north with a moving company, with the plan of meeting the truck at our new home in four days' time. Our final weekend in Berkeley was spent in a local hotel, while we visited family in the area for one last time. We boarded another flight to Seattle on the evening of November 26, this time with Zach assigned to his mother's supervision. By the time we arrived, our report on the results of Payload Systems' second round of crystallization experiments on the *Mir* space station had just appeared in the latest edition of *Nature*. It would be a noteworthy start to my career as an assistant professor at the Fred Hutchinson Cancer Research Center.

# TAPPING OUT

### YELTSIN CRUSHES REVOLT

Jonathan Steele and David Hearst reporting in *The Guardian*, Tuesday, October 5, 1993

President Boris Yeltsin moved swiftly last night to stamp his absolute power on Russia by suspending a range of political movements and closing opposition newspapers after the surrender of his main parliamentary opponents in the wake of the assault on the Russian White House. Under a decree following the state of emergency that Mr. Yeltsin imposed on Sunday, the National Salvation Front, the Russian Communist Party, the United Front of Workers and the Union of Officers were banned, while Pravda, the former organ of the Soviet Communist Party, and a number of other papers were told to cease publication. An overnight curfew was also imposed throughout Moscow.

After a grisly 10-hour gun battle in which tanks punched holes in the front of the White House, all but an unknown number of last-ditch snipers surrendered. The indiscriminate exchanges of fire left hundreds injured and an unknown number of dead. The assault set fire to the riverside front of the building and reduced whole floors to rubble. Earlier in the day, a brief but fierce exchange took place about 200 yards along the embankment, and tank artillery was blamed for starting a fire at the Mezhdunarodnaya hotel.

I watched the news broadcasts of the open warfare in the streets of Moscow, which had played out over the past forty-eight hours, with wide eyes and a deepening sense of dread. I was only ten months into my new position at the Hutch and was still involved in organizing the upcoming future missions to *Mir* that were being planned by Payload Systems. I had agreed to send my newly hired staff scientist to Russia and Kazakhstan in my place. Her flight out to Moscow was scheduled to leave in only two days. Balanced against her planned travel were news clips and videos of running gun battles and tanks on the streets of Moscow. There was no way that I could allow an employee under my supervision to travel into such a situation, even if the immediate threat had been violently and successfully squashed by the Russian President. I considered the option of stepping in myself to set up the experiments. As I pondered the idea, I gradually realized and then decisively concluded that it would not happen. My time as an unlikely space scientist was coming to a very sudden end.

Our arrival in Seattle had coincided with the onset of a typical dark, stormy Seattle winter as well as the impending installation of the first Democrat administration in the White House since my senior year in high school. I had spent my first month at the Hutchinson Center holed up at a desk at the Hutch's original research space, which would soon be abandoned for a new campus slightly north of downtown. Of the four research divisions at the Hutch at that time, the one into which I had been hired (generically called "Basic Sciences") would be one of the first two to occupy the newly constructed buildings.

The first wave of laboratory moves was scheduled for early spring of 1993, but I was given keys and access to the building immediately after the new year, to receive an incoming delivery of brand-new X-ray equipment and participate in its installation. For the first three months of 1993, I occupied a laboratory space that had been finished ahead of schedule and would be equipped only with a laptop and a new X-ray generator and detector. Even furniture would have to catch up with me; until its delivery I sat on a wooden crate that had contained a high voltage transformer that powered the X-ray generator. During those days I had no telephone, no email, and no internet; while at work I was cut off from the world and the world was cut off from me. Those were, without a doubt, some of the very best months of my entire career.

Less than three weeks after I gained access to my new lab space, the area was hit by a windstorm of historical proportions on January 20. Quickly dubbed the Inauguration Day Storm, the sudden onslaught of sustained winds of up to seventy miles per hour came with little or no warning. By the time the storm relented, hours later, dozens of homes were destroyed, five people were dead, and power was lost at almost a million residences throughout the area, including our own house. To complicate matters, the temperature throughout the region swiftly dropped to well below freezing. By the morning after the storm, our house became exceedingly uncomfortable; we realized that our new home had virtually no insulation. The four of us resorted to sleeping together in the living room in front of our fireplace.

Responding to the situation with a level of self-centered unawareness that astounds me to this day, I continued to go to work and left Amy alone each subsequent day with our two toddlers, in a powerless neighborhood where she had yet to meet anyone. The boys responded within a day by both contracting a stomach virus; soon our bathtub was filled with soiled clothes and bedding that would need to wait for restoration of power before being washed. By that Friday evening, I came to my senses and realized that the living situation at home, not to mention the state of my marriage, was becoming grim.

Rather than subject the family to another night in the cold and dark, I booked a hotel down the street from the Hutch, and by that evening we were all enjoying bright lights, hot showers, and warm beds. The next day saw the restoration of our power and a corresponding rapid improvement in my marital polling numbers and political standing.

I had been concerned about the reception of our pointed commentary that had been published two months earlier. In that piece, entitled *"Mir* for the crystallographers' money,"* we had indicated, in a somewhat understated but quite clear manner, that we found the descriptions of space-based crystallization that had been put forward by investigators working with NASA to be overblown. I was not eager to start my career by picking a fight with a group of vastly more senior research faculty than myself, not to mention the entire US space agency. Shortly after arriving in Seattle, I had queried Anthony about the response within the space science community; he informed me that the only feedback that he had received in response to the article had been to its final paragraph. At the conclusion of our commentary, we had touted the performance of the Russian space program and the *Mir* space station, stating:

> *Mir* is as good a microgravity platform as the Shuttle. Because the Russian launch vehicle which delivers our experiments to Mir is unmanned, we have found that sending experiments to the space station is more reliable than trying to do similar experiments on the Shuttle. Finally, because Mir is a permanently orbiting space station, we can do long-duration experiments that are not possible on any other microgravity platform. It is clear that researchers in the West should consider using Mir for their microgravity experiments. Given the uncertainties over continued funding for the Mir program in Russia, such collaboration would clearly be of mutual benefit for crystallographers.

We had preceded that concluding paragraph by stating, "We hope that readers with proteins which may be appropriate for such experiments will contact us." Officials in the US space flight program had focused almost entirely on that statement, appearing to read it as a blatant attempt to siphon away interest and investment in their own program, as well as potential future industrial partnerships. They had either missed or deliberately ignored the preceding implication that the actual value of zero-gravity crystallization to the structural biology research community was minimal.

After the final breakup of the Soviet Union at the end of 1991 and subsequent installation of a new government headed by Boris Yeltsin, along with groundbreaking economic and political reforms, Russia had been steadily lurching towards a constitutional crisis and violent confrontation between the old and new guard. Unsurprisingly, the collapse of communism had immediately led to a corresponding collapse in the Russian economy, with unemployment skyrocketing, industries that had previously been propped up by the regime collapsing, and unpopular new taxes being levied on a population whose earnings had plummeted. By the end of 1992 and continuing into the following year, the Russian parliament and the presidency were in open conflict over the direction of the country and the nature of power-sharing in the newly formed government. The situation came to a head on September 21, 1993 (just weeks before Payload Systems and its research team were due to return for the third mission to Baikonur), when Boris Yeltsin declared the Congress of People's Deputies and the Supreme Soviet were to be dissolved.

Within days, tens of thousands of Moscow residents were marching in the streets, protesting the deteriorating conditions in the country and Yeltsin's actions. Within a week, the Parliament building was occupied by hundreds of members of a well-armed militia in support of the anti-Yeltsin opposition; the Kremlin responded by barricading and isolating the structure. Within another week, large number of additional forces, including units from the military, had crossed the barricades, and joined together in armed opposition. On October 3, 1993, the city of Moscow fell into open street warfare, now referred to as the "second October Revolution." By time the fighting was over, one hundred forty-five civilians and soldiers were dead, the top floors of the Parliament building were reduced to smoldering wreckage from the shelling by tanks, and hundreds of supporters of the parliament had been arrested and marched away. The majority are thought to have been summarily executed.

Shortly before the storming of the Parliament building commenced, Yeltsin had issued a chilling declaration of his intent:

> Those who went against the peaceful city and unleashed bloody slaughter are criminals. Everything that took place and is still taking place in Moscow is a pre-planned armed rebellion. It has been organized by Communists, Fascist leaders, former deputies, and the representatives of the Soviets. Under the cover of negotiations, they gathered forces and recruited bandit troops who were accustomed to murder and violence. A petty gang of politicians attempted by armed force to impose their will on the entire country. Those who are waving red flags have again stained Russia with blood. The fascist-communist armed rebellion in Moscow therefore shall be suppressed within the shortest period.

At the same time, in the distant Russian city of Saint Petersburg, a low-level political bureaucrat in the mayor's office, tasked with promoting foreign investments in the city and its industries, came under investigation for price fixing and corruption, leading to a recommendation he be fired. Despite that challenge, he would remain in his position and continue his methodical climb up the Russian political ladder. His name was Vladimir Putin.

Unlike prior strife in the region, the carnage across Moscow during the fall of 1993 had been broadcast live and in living color into households throughout the world, including my own. Watching the news broadcasts, I recognized some of the streets that I had strolled where the most intense fighting and bloodshed had occurred. The next morning, I placed a call to Payload Systems and spoke at length with its CEO. Despite his mild protests, I held to my conviction that the results that we were obtaining were not worth the risk of traveling again to the former Soviet Union anytime in the coming days, nor worth the trouble and expense in years to come. We decided on a new course of action for the final mission; the devices would be loaded in our laboratories in the States, and then transported to Baikonur under the care of Payload Systems engineers, to be directly handed over to Russian counterparts for launch. We would take possession of the devices upon their return and complete our participation in the program with one final examination of those crystals that had grown. We agreed that that would be the end of our work together.

With that, we wished each other well and hung up on the call. *Crystals in Space, Ltd.* had arrived at its end, and with it the short, unexpected space research career of the Baikonur Man.

# EPILOGUE

**TEN YEARS OF** microgravity crystallization experiments, covering over 100 protein species and using several different microgravity platforms, indicates that there has yet to be a single crystallization project which has yielded any major improvement leading to significant structural information which could not be attained through ground-based methodologies at lower cost. It is therefore worthwhile to perform a cost-benefit analysis of microgravity-based crystallization.

The take-home message of this analysis is clear: space-based research, while important in its own right as a driving force for technological innovation, cannot and should not be justified by relationships with well-established research areas, such as structural biology, which actually derive few benefits from manned space programs.

It is clear that the greater the potential cost of a research program to a nation, the greater the need for impartial peer review, criticism, and policy advisement from a broad spectrum of the most well-respected and productive investigators in that particular research field, in order to maintain accountability among all involved agencies and investigators.

—From "The facts and fancy of microgravity protein crystallization" by Barry Stoddard, Gregory Farber, and Roland Strong, published in *Biotechnology and Genetic Engineering Reviews* in December 1993

I finally decided, with the agreement of the company, to end to my involvement in the Payload Systems project in the fall of 1993, as did Roland and Greg. However, the three of us had already come to firm agreement on the value of space-based protein crystallization well before that and had committed to put our thoughts into writing that year. Exactly four years since we had first departed Boston for the Soviet Union, our opinions were published for the larger research community to read and discuss. There were no significant disagreements or arguments raised within the protein crystallography community. Even those who had been involved for the past ten years with similar experiments on the US Shuttle program did not raise an objection.

In the end, the theory that crystal growth itself might be enhanced by the absence of gravity was (and still is) completely valid. However, the concept that the effects of zero gravity would enable significant advances in protein crystallography was undone by a simple fact—the growth of protein crystals is vastly more dependent on efforts in the laboratory to optimize the molecules prior to setting up crystallization experiments (and then on multiple, time-consuming rounds of crystallization trials to optimize growth conditions) than it is on the alteration of a single environmental variable, even one as fundamentally important as gravity. Hopes that protein crystallization in space would become a game-changing technology hit a brick wall not because the concept was flawed, but because its successful execution required that all the steps in the laboratory that lead to successful crystal growth be transferred to space and carried out with the same attention to detail that was applied on Earth. In the end, transferring an entire crystallography lab to orbit and then pursuing individual projects for month after month was simply not feasible.

Well over thirty years later, to the best of my knowledge, not one single protein structure has been solved due solely or even primarily to the availability of space-grown crystals.

**Payload Systems Inc** completed its third and final mission to *Mir* in the fall of 1993, transporting the last crystallization experiments back to the US two months later. The company then terminated the project and returned to working with NASA as they placed commercial scientific payloads on the renewed Shuttle program and eventually on the International Space Station. In 2007, Payload was acquired by Aurora Flights Sciences Corporation and merged with that company's flight sciences division.

**The US Space Shuttle program** flew one hundred thirty-five missions over its thirty-year history, before finally being retired in 2011. A second shuttle and its entire crew were also lost during that time, when the *Columbia* was destroyed during its reentry into the Earth's atmosphere in 2003. Since the end of the Shuttle program, its original duties have been taken over by a variety of private and government-sponsored space flight vessels, including the European Automated Transfer Vehicle, the US Airforce X-37B space plane, commercial spacecraft launched by Space-X and Orbital Sciences, and the continued launch of Soyuz capsules by the Russian space program.

**Lawrence Mulloy,** who served as the project manager for the Space Shuttle Solid Rocket Booster Program at the time of the Challenger disaster, was a defendant in a multimillion-dollar lawsuit filed on behalf of the families of the shuttle crew. Singled out for being particularly responsible for the tragedy, he retired only a few months after the explosion and afterward lived quietly and anonymously in Tennessee.

**NASA's KC-135 parabolic, zero-gravity bounce flights, still**

referred to as the Vomit Comet, continue to fly from Ellington Field in Houston and challenge the hardware, stomachs, and fortitude of all newcomers and veterans of space-based research. It made its Hollywood debut by providing zero gravity for scenes filmed as part of the Hollywood film *Apollo 13*.

The Buran spaceplane never flew again after its sole unmanned mission. The Russian shuttle program was terminated in 1993 by order of Boris Yeltsin, after an investment of twenty billion rubles. Ten years after our second mission, in 2002, Buran was destroyed when the roof of the storage building that we had visited collapsed due to corrosion and poor maintenance. The accident killed eight Baikonur staff who were in the building at the time. Two partially constructed and similarly abandoned shuttles continue to accumulate dust and rust while sitting in storage at other Russian space facilities.

The *Mir* space station continued to orbit until 2001, when funding for its continued habitation, supplies, and maintenance finally ran out. From its initial assembly in orbit in 1986 until its abandonment fifteen years later, it was continuously crewed for most of its time in orbit, and still holds the record for the longest continuous single human space flight, with Valeri Polyakov spending 437 days and eighteen hours on the station during 1994 and 1995. In February 1997, the space station suffered a fire started by a malfunctioning oxygen generator, followed three months later by an accidental collision with an incoming unmanned supply rocket that ripped a hole in the side of one of its sections. Amazingly, nobody on board the space station died in either incident and *Mir* continued to orbit for an additional four years. In 2001, the space station was deliberately brought down from its orbit, burning up in the atmosphere over the South Pacific Ocean in a matter of minutes. Roland and I drank a toast to its memory and the role it had played in our younger lives. We chose an excellent scotch from Roland's extensive collection, rather than Armenian cognac, for that purpose.

Fujitsu Incorporated never got back in touch with us about

their crystallization trials from mission number two. True to their word, they also never asked for the pink thermos to be returned to them. They did, however, continue to work towards the development and commercialization of computer-assisted drug design tools, culminating in the description of the quantum-inspired digital annealer for drug design. That tool was described in a recent publication from the company as *"a heuristic technique for solving hard optimization problems by mimicking quantum mechanical effects such as quantum tunneling, which is a promising approach."* While the author of this book has absolutely no idea what that means, it sounds science-y as heck and so has his approval.

**Congressman Bill Nelson** of Florida was the second sitting member of the US congress to fly in space (preceded by Senator Jake Garn of Utah). The STS-61-C mission on which he flew was the final flight before the Challenger disaster. He retired from Congress shortly after our return from the first mission to Kazakhstan to run, unsuccessfully, for governor of Florida. After ten years in various elected state offices (including the post of state Fire Marshal), he served as a US senator from 2000 to 2018. In 2021, he was nominated to become the fourteenth Administrator of NASA and serves in that capacity today.

**Boris Yeltsin** served as the president of Russia from the end of 1991 until his resignation on the final day of 1999. Despite initial success and praise in driving the final collapse of the Soviet state and introducing a market economy to the newly formed Russian state, he failed to prevent the transfer of a significant amount of formerly state-controlled resources, industry, and wealth into the hands of small number of oligarchs, and the eventual descent of Russia into political chaos from which its next murderous leader would rise and eventually threaten the security and future of human civilization. Yeltsin eventually became reviled throughout the country as it slid into political and economic chaos. He died in 2007, after years of physical and mental decay rumored to be accelerated by lifelong alcoholism.

The mid-level KGB functionary and regional politician mentioned twice in this book, **Vladimir Putin**, moved to Moscow and joined the Yeltsin administration in 1996. He was appointed to the role of Prime Minister in August 1999 and then became president of Russia in 2000, upon the resignation of Yeltsin. He has served continuously as president or prime minister every year since, and during that time has ordered military operations in Chechnya, Georgia, Syria, and the Ukraine, culminating with the full-fledged catastrophic invasion of that latter country in February of 2022.

**Greg Petsko** continued to thrive as a renowned research investigator after his move to Brandeis University at the end of 1989. He was named to the National Academy of Sciences, the National Academy of Medicine, the American Academy of Arts and Sciences, and the American Philosophical Society. He is currently professor of neurology at the Ann Romney Center for Neurologic Diseases at Harvard Medical School and Brigham and Women's Hospital. In addition to myself, Roland, and Greg, many other graduate students and postdoctoral fellows who worked in his laboratory and learned from Greg went on to faculty positions and research careers throughout the world.

**Daniel Koshland** ran a large and productive lab for another fifteen years after I left Berkeley, continuing to develop new scientific interests and exciting directions for research to the very end. One of the final projects that he introduced to his lab focused on the development and characterization of cyanobacteria for potential use as biofuel generating microbes. In 1992, a research building on the UC-Berkeley campus was named after him, marking the first time in that school's history that such an honor was bestowed on an active and still living faculty member. Dan passed away in July of 2007, at age eighty-seven, while still working full time as a research professor. Despite his oft-stated desire to drop dead in the middle of the lab while engaged in a lively scientific debate with one of his postdoctoral fellows, he instead succumbed to the effects of a massive stroke suffered while tending his garden on a beautiful Saturday morning.

**Charles Stoddard,** my father and proud former officer in the US Army Corps of Engineers 35th Combat Battalion, spent the remainder of his working civilian life in the forest products industry. After moving to the Seattle area, he consulted regularly for the United States Navy, putting the combination of his expertise in wood and lumber, along with his still active clearance in nuclear weaponry to good use during annual inspections of Trident submarine enclosures (which are constructed entirely from treated wood) located at the Bangor Naval Base on the Washington Coast. One of the last socially moderate, honest conservatives, he passed away in early 2019, thankfully spared from having to live through COVID and the events of January 6th, 2020.

**Amy Stoddard** stuck with the author of this book through thick and thin, even during the dark days of their first winter in Seattle. After raising two boys with occasional assistance from her husband and spending twenty years working in a special education program within the local public school district (where she supported students on the autism spectrum), she took a well-deserved early retirement to focus on family, friends, workouts, and gardening.

**Mark Hawthorne, the "Hate Man,"** continued to live on the streets of Berkeley and to harass street preachers until his death at the age of eighty. Despite advancing age and deteriorating health, he steadfastly chose to live a life of a homeless man until the very end, when congestive heart failure forced a final hospitalization and subsequent stay in a nursing facility. He was quoted near the end of his life stating, "I'm a lot like Jesus, except I give out cigarettes instead of miracles."

**Andrew Martinez, a.k.a. "the Naked Guy"** was expelled from the University of California near the end of 1992 just as we were leaving Berkeley. Fourteen years later, having been diagnosed with schizophrenia, he committed suicide in a Santa Clara jail.

**Anthony Arrott, Jr.,** pursued a wide-ranging career in

information technology after leaving Payload Systems, including a consulting practice focused on satellite communications and imaging technologies, participating in internet gaming startups during the early dot com era, and working in market analytics and digital threat research for the security software industry. He is currently a retired business owner who continues to serve as a senior partner for multiple cybersecurity firms.

**Byron Lichtenberg**, who co-founded Payload Systems with Anthony, is a professor at LeTourneau University in Longview Texas, and the Chief Technical Officer of the Zero Gravity Corporation, which provides parabolic bounce flights for a fee out of Fort Lauderdale, Florida. Founded in 2004, nearly twenty thousand paying customers, including celebrities such as Penn and Teller, Martha Stewart, Tony Hawk, Adam Savage and Stephen Hawking, have paid several thousand dollars to throw up during multiple interludes of zero gravity parabolas.

**Jeff Manber** went on from working at the US Department of Commerce and assisting Payload Systems to become the managing director of Energia Ltd, which represented the Russian space company NPO Energia to foreign interests. There, he worked to market the Russian space program as a potential partner both to NASA and to a wide variety of US aerospace firms. Since 2009, he has been the CEO of NanoRacks, which provides hardware and services for the deployment of payloads to the International Space Station. He was the author of the 2009 book *Selling Peace: Inside the Soviet Conspiracy that Transformed the US Space Program*. Much of the information provided in this book about how Payload Systems negotiated a contract with the Russians and an export license from the US government was shamelessly extracted from his excellent narrative.

**Julianne Zimmerman** also survived her time in Kazakhstan and our night of epic drinking with our Russian hosts; I imagine she still possesses an aversion to the smell of cognac that rivals my own. She left Payload systems after fourteen years as a field engineer and moved on to a long and fruitful career as a member, founder, mentor, and advisor to many different, mostly technology-driven startup companies. She is a managing director of a Capital Venture firm that invests exclusively in US-based companies founded and led by BIPOC (black, indigenous and people of color) individuals.

**Maria Douglass** left Payload Systems shortly after the end of the Crystals in Space program and went on to a successful career working at the intersection of technology and business, much of it focused on commercial business opportunities in Russia and the redirection of military industries there into privatized research and development opportunities. After years working with the Kingdom of Saudi Arabia, she became involved in Silicon Valley startups involved in alternative information technology platforms. As far as I am aware, she never again was put behind the controls of a jet airliner.

**Chris Krebs** and **Bob Renshaw** both remained at Payload Systems and then Aurora Flight Sciences Corporation; Bob remained at that company as a project manager, while Chris eventually became a principal engineer at Accion Systems Inc. in the Boston area. I assume their palates and dietary preferences were permanently affected by day after day after day of nonstop beet-centered meals just as much as mine was.

**Aleksandr Viktoenko** and **Aleksandr Serebrov**, the two cosmonauts who handled, operated, and returned our first experiments, flew multiple missions to the Soviet space station and eventually accumulated 489 and 372 days in space, respectively. For many years, Serebrov held the record for most spacewalks and was also known for carrying along and playing *Tetris* on a Nintendo Game Boy aboard the *Mir* space station, thereby achieving another Russian first in space exploration history.

**William Broad** continued his career as a science writer, author, and senior writer at the *New York Times*. His writing resume includes eight books including a number one *New York Times* best-seller entitled *Germs: Biological Weapons and America's Secret*

*War.* He has shared in two Pulitzer Prizes and won an Emmy award. He cited *New York Times* policy against providing accolades for books when asked to do so for *Baikonur Man*, stating in an email to the author, "It sounds lovely . . . I hope it soars. We need tales of cooperation more than ever, no?"

**Various members of the Petsko lab from the late 1980s and the Koshland lab of the early 1990s,** in addition to myself, Greg, and Roland, went on to become professors at universities and research institutions all around the country and beyond, including Rockefeller University, University of California-Berkeley, Albert Einstein University, Yale, the University of North Carolina, the University of Toronto, and the Max Planck Institute in Germany.

**Greg Farber** left Pennsylvania State University in the summer of 2000, shortly after receiving tenure in its biochemistry department. He joined the NIH and began to pursue a career in science administration, working for ten years at the National Center for Research Resources and then becoming the director of the Office of Technology Development and Coordination at the National Institute of Mental Health.

**Roland Strong** completed his postdoctoral research fellowship at the California Institute of Technology, and then joined the faculty at the Fred Hutchinson Cancer Center in Seattle in early 1994, where he has run a laboratory next to mine for the past twenty-seven years. Like me, he continues to utilize crystallography as one of his primary approaches to the study of protein structure and function, focusing almost entirely on human immunology, cancer immunotherapy, and vaccine development. He and I have often entertained our trainees, colleagues, and each other with stories of our trials and adventures in Moscow and Kazakhstan. Just as this book was being readied for publication, he suffered a massive heart attack and was clinically dead for a brief period; through the heroic resuscitation efforts by his partner and first responders, followed by the efforts of dedicated nurses and doctors at the University of

Washington hospital, he survived and now continues to entertain me and our labs with his humor, sarcasm, and overall good nature.

**The US space science industry** has never stopped marketing microgravity as being extremely important for protein crystallography. A flyer recently put out by a firm which helps manage the International Space Station US national laboratory for NASA, states that "Macromolecular crystallization in space produces large, well-ordered crystals, allowing determination of detailed structures, including therapeutically important domains and binding sites."

The author of this book, **Barry Stoddard,** still lives in Bellevue, Washington, with his wife, Amy. His boys (**Ben** and **Zach**) both grew up to become engineers (computers and aerospace, respectively) and terrific young men. Barry still runs a research laboratory at the Fred Hutchinson Cancer Center (in his opinion an absolutely perfect institution at which to pursue a career in research) and is also the senior editor of the journal *Nucleic Acids Research.* In his spare time, he enjoys reading, traveling, theater, music, skiing, golfing, diving, drinking good wine and interesting cocktails, and eating virtually anything (except olives, lentils, and to this very day especially beets). He has always been willing to try anything interesting at least once and has yet to regret doing so. Among the many adventures that his career in science has brought into his life, his time working with Payload Systems and the Soviet and Russian space program remains at the very top of the list.

# ACKNOWLEDGMENTS

**THIS BOOK WOULD** never have come to fruition without the seminal contribution of the SARS COVID-19 virus, which successfully executed a zoonotic transfer into the human population sometime in late 2019, and eventually drove me out of the lab and into involuntary home confinement in early 2020. Faced with the prospect of days and then weeks without access to my lab, I decided to put my fingers to a keyboard and assemble my stories about MIT, Berkeley, Payload Systems, Russia, Kazakhstan, and the Soviet space program into the narrative you just read.

Beyond the critical contribution of the novel coronavirus to this book, I thank my outstanding editor Elizabeth Stansell, and the staff at Koehler Books for shepherding both myself and this book through the process of writing, polishing, and publishing this tale. As well, many thanks to the current and former members of my research laboratory and many friends and family members over the years who not only listened to my stories about Baikonur Man and crystals in space, but who also encouraged me to organize those stories into this narrative.

Finally, as mentioned earlier much of the information in this book about how Payload Systems managed to navigate the US and Soviet bureaucracies of the day and form a partnership with our Russian counterparts, found largely in the chapter entitled "Bureaucrats, Russians, Lawyers and Congressmen," was derived and adapted from the book *Selling Peace* by Jeff Manber, and from an article and corresponding interviews that were written up and posted at the Fred Hutch online news feed by Susan Keown in 2014 (on the 25th anniversary of the first mission).

Ingram Content Group UK Ltd.
Milton Keynes UK
UKHW041042300323
419409UK00003B/101

9 781646 639427